Unholy Melodies

New & Collected

Also by Ted Jonathan

Spiked Libido (1998)

Bones & Jokes (2009)

Run (2016)

Unholy Melodies

New & Collected

Ted Jonathan

The New York Quarterly Foundation, Inc.
Beacon, New York

NYQ Books™ is an imprint of The New York Quarterly Foundation, Inc.

The New York Quarterly Foundation, Inc.
P. O. Box 470
Beacon, NY 12508

www.nyq.org

First Edition

Set in New Baskerville

Layout and Design by Raymond P. Hammond

Library of Congress Control Number: 2021941074

ISBN: 978-1-63045-91-5

Unholy Melodies

New & Collected

Contents

Run

High Noon at Midnight:

Unholy Melodies

Foreword

Tony Gloeggler

I first met Ted Jonathan at a reading for *Skidrow Penthouse*, 2007 maybe. We both had work in the current issue, and there was an afternoon reading in someone's Manhattan apartment near Washington Square Park. I didn't know anybody except one of the editors, a friend of an ex girlfriend, Joshua's mom, and I was looking to make a quick getaway. I had liked what Ted had read and told him so, and he said he had liked my work for years in NYQ. He was real close with the editor and his mentor Bill Packard who was my most important poetry teacher. Anyway, we ended up at a diner for a few hours.

Had he started with turkey burgers back then, or was he still ordering real hamburger specials? He was dealing with cancer shit, and I'm not sure whether it was at the start, middle, or end, whether it was Cancer #1 or #2. I do remember it had something to do with his throat. I'm sure we talked poetry, Bill/NYQ, sports and music, and probably the poets who had read—the few we liked, the many we didn't. Pretty much our life long conversation if you add old girlfriends, my work, my connection to Joshua, our very different childhoods, the silliness of the poetry world. I knew pretty quickly he was a guy it would be good for me to know. As usual, I was right, and we became close friends. We were both neighborhood guys, though his was tougher; his life was even rougher than the Bronx in the crack years. But we both surprisingly ended up writing poetry and thinking it mattered. Probably more so to him. He'd tell me how it saved his life and he was happiest when writing.

We started exchanging poems, and I doubt we have written anything that we didn't show each other for at least ten years. I'd send him my first final version and, only if he asked, the version I'd submit around. He'd send me five to ten versions and then two years later he'd send me an email saying he worked over an old one and finally got it right. Sometimes, the changes were miniscule, and I'd say it's the same damn poem, leave it alone, you're just gonna fuck it up. Sometimes, I'd tell him he was right for the first time. But he worked hard chiseling away at his poems. Never stopped.

I've always dug Ted's work a great deal, always felt he had a unique voice that very much matched his personality. Blunt, straightforward, take-no prisoners kind of stuff with a demented sense of humor touched by his charm and big heart. He has this punchy rhythm that I once described as a boxer working a heavy bag, powerful blows with a lot of stops and starts followed by unanticipated combinations and surprising sound play. His words were conversational, everyday language. But the rhythm was more like Tarzan and Jane having an argument, especially in his early work. He was a master at the rant, except his rants never seemed to run on endlessly, backed by a steady, driving rhythm. His rants were calculated, contained, focused and had a pissed off attitude and a sense that this could get dangerous. He was shoving his finger into your face, poking your eyeballs with a list of points that stung and at the same time made you laugh hard enough until stuff came out of your nose.

His poems explored his darkness, a lot of what was taken from him, what he missed out on and hardly any of the poems turn out good or happy. He portrayed scenes and situations that seemed plucked from his life and he told them honestly, the way he remembered them. There was never a sense that he was looking for sympathy or any attempt to come across as a good guy. But it was clear he was a good guy and the more you got to know him, the better man he seemed to be. He had a strong code of ethics and took responsibility in his poems and in his life, which is something I admire and try to emulate.

As much as I enjoy Ted on the page, his poems grew more powerful, funnier and more poignant when he was on a stage and they were coming out of his mouth. He had a deep voice he was proud to show off and just owned a stage. I think he felt most at home, most comfortable up there, like he was untouchable. He had this swagger, this I-can-say-fucking-anything attitude and I don't give a shit what anybody thinks, and everybody loved it. He'd get to the mic and maybe make a production of taking off his glasses slowly, clearing his throat with a guttural sound that shook the walls, taking a long drink of water that he usually followed with the latest thing that pissed him off on his way to the venue that somehow ended up being hilarious. He'd then wind through his narratives filled with lines that startled you with gut punches and left you with this tender ache that throbbed with a core of pure truth.

Yes, I will miss the poems he would have kept writing, sitting in the audience at a Ted Jonathan reading, but mostly I will miss sitting in a diner disagreeing, arguing about everything, and cracking on each other constantly. I've spoken to, emailed with a lot of folks who know him well, and they all feel a big loss. He was a positive force in a lot of people's lives; his death hurts a lot of us and really just fucking sucks.

I do hope Ted knew that so many people cared about him, loved him, and that I was one of them. I know I will miss him too often.

—Tony Gloeggler
New York City
2021

Spiked Libido

Neukeia Press, 1998

spiked
libido

ten poems & one story
by **Ted Jonathan**

with a foreword by **William Packard**

"IN THESE UTTERLY ORIGINAL POEMS, TED JONATHAN
has created New York City street scenes and
street characters that are alarmingly fresh
and frighteningly unique. Even the arbitrary
punctuation of these poems adds to the dense
texture of violence and immediate need which is
the pain and dissonance of contemporary life
in the Bronx.

Behind the profanity and quick switchblade diction
of these poems, there is a gentle love and clear sanity
that makes the poetry permanently memorable."

—William Packard

   author of *Saturday Night at San Marcos*/Grove Press, Inc.;
   The Poet's Dictionary/Harper & Row; and
   The Art of Poetry Writing/St. Martin's Press

Ted Jonathan is 43. A lifelong Bronx resident,
he is a graduate of Lehman College. His poetry
has appeared in *The New York Quarterly*. This
chapbook is his first.

spiked
libido

spiked
libido

For Raymond Hammond —

ten poems & one story

by **Ted Jonathan**

Ted Jonathan
4/28/98

Neukeia Press
New York

The following poems have appeared in *The New York Quarterly:*

Son of Sam
Tommy Bolan
These Words are of No Help to Holly

First Edition

Copyright ©1998 by Ted Jonathan.

Design and typography by Mark Hayes.
Printing and binding by Wayne Yee.
Photos by Erik La Prade.
Manufactured in the United States of America.

Monotype Century Schoolbook is primary typeface with Courier
as secondary typeface. Reproduction proofs output on QMS 1660.
Printed using Kodak HVP Imaging System.

Published by Neukeia Press, New York.
First Printing March 1998.
Limited edition of 300 copies.

contents

Son of Sam

Clapping, he'd look around; at the other boys on
his side of the volleyball court who were clapping.
When they stopped, he stopped.

Burly, friendless, and blank,—

Berkowitz. In black dress socks, gym shorts, and
sneakers. Back in high school gym class.

Spent a couple years as a peacetime soldier, and moved
on to become a nighttime postal worker; before he got
busted for being—

Son of Sam. Girl hunter who'd thunder them bloody with
his 44. A self-described, "chubby behemoth." Who heard
his killing orders in the—

Barking. Out his window. In the alley. Sam Carr's dog—
BARKING BARKING BARKING BARKING—

Berkowitz. Showed you. Chose to. Show you.
KILLING KILLING KILLING KILLING—

BREATH-ING!

1

Myles Spenser

I passed out; dead. OD'ed on dope; at 23. My powerful, round body, was carried out of the shooting gallery; into the south Bronx sunlight; laid out by the front stoop; and abandoned. One block from where I grew up.

My old man loved dope. He got off dope, and on methadone about a year ago—when the program began. He got a job—driving a limo. My mother hollered a lot. She was heavy into Bingo. I got one, younger brother. He's on methadone. I tried to throw him out a window when his girlfriend told me he pissed on her. I don't remember—ever—caring about any of them.

The year I turned 23, we moved to a better neighborhood. There, I met Donny. I dug him: handed him a bag of pot, and told him to take as much as he wanted; told him how the hit-and-run left me with a steel-pin in my hip, and glass-eye; and, that if anyone ever bothered him, to let me know— because I don't expect to make 25.

I fucked-up a huge, asshole football player; outside a club. I fucked-up a pimp, poolside; in Miami. I let Eddie Thomas get the better of me; because I liked him, and he was right.

I ate it up; when Donny and the guys said how great I was, and I loved; to hear my deep sweet voice talk them up.

The guys shot dope. I dove in. I ripped-off a dealer. Pulled him right out from behind the wheel of his car. We all got-off on the roof. I mugged an old man, bloodied his fine, blue pinstriped, Sunday suit.

I shot big hits. The day my dead body was found, I shot a lot of good-shit.

2

Hearts to Clubs

"I'm out,"

says Milt: the father of our host, as he folds his cards.
Bloated and wasted. In his fifties. He's about thirty years older,
than me, and the three other players seated around the table.
He turns to his son who's still in. He tells him:

"Ya dunno watda fuck ya doin an' it's fuckin me up."

His son doesn't even look at him. He's locked in on the pot.
Milt splashes some cologne on his scalp, and combs his three
hairs: straight back. Broke. He rises. And heads to the toilet.

*Seven card poker. In the single-room, Bronx, basement apartment.
On the bicentennial.*

Campbell deals the final round, down. Clockwise, to those
players still in the pot: our host, Philip, me, and himself.
Our host pulls his cards slow and opens with a buck bet.
Looks left at who's next—and says to him:

"It's to you Philip fuckinRetard."

Philip laughs nervously. He babbles. Campbell yells at him:

"Shutdafuckup."

He does. But not before he ups the bet another buck.
It's to me.
There's about forty bucks in the pot.
I need to squeeze a heart for a flush—any heart—I need to squeeze
a heart—a heart to the hearts—a heart to the hearts—a heart—

"Ya inna out?"
—Clubs—

3

Mirrored

A small
boy.
In the tall hall mirror.
The one on the front
of the closet door.
The mirror his
father would
admire himself in.

Having to piss—the boy
turns his head left, to
face the toilet door down
the hall
waiting, for
It to swing open—

It swung open—

foam faced white
—father—
bare muscled right
arm hangs from chin
white sleeveless shaver
in hand hisses
lithuanian strangled
fatherly
advice:

"A pimple sha-veoff."

4

Broken Reunion

You cried in class; when President Kennedy was shot.

A very smart girl, with blonde curls. In a third grade
class filled with smart kids.

I was put into that class: made friends; you were in love
with me; I was elected class president. Maybe, someday;
you'd be my girlfriend.

So, when I looked to see who was calling me, I knew it was
you. Even though, fifteen years had since passed.

At your apartment in Hoboken; you told me you had gone to
college in Oneonta, and left to hook-up with the Hare Krish-
nas. You got naked, and blasted a fart. You said you wanted
to suck my toes, and looked to me for your cue to start.

While I thought: my feet are unwashed, I need more tuinals,
did I run over that cop's foot?, I can only do it with whores.

Lit a cigarette. Got up, and left.

5

what terrors fell buried?

when she
—was—
a soft-boned
girlchild—

cough-fire
in her—stomach
        chest—
headaches—
left gulping for air—

wears—a
large gray sweatshirt
to hide
large breasts—

hardly goes outside—

6

ChickenMen

a massive body lay passive on bronx pavement
dull--yellow--limbless--it was a massive plucked chicken--
its head--that of a weathered gray man--
chin rests on pavement head upright mouth gulps air--

a lump of human shit before him--fills him with
hunger and lust--shit--he--and another like him who
lies alongside him are set to de-
vour--on this sidewalk crowded with women some
with children--none are sickened by the chickenmen

I am--I take on shame--chickenmen--feel no feelings--
a fine demure light black lady look-
alike for young mary tyler moore acts ta-
ken aback--same as she would if she was across
the street--where a younger chickenman is set to eat

7

Tommy Bolan

The raggy, rage-filled voice of my father spasmed noise
to match the noise made, as he harshly shoved kitchen
furniture on the linoleum floor—

    to get to mom?

I—was a little kid, in the darkness of my bed—her cries
were muffled—the door stayed closed, I couldn't sleep—

    was he hitting her?

My little sister slept in the other bed. It was the only
bedroom of the 3 room apartment. On the other side of the
shut door was a small foyer. To the left was the bathroom.
On the right was the doorless arched entrance to the living
room—where our parents would sleep on the sofabed. You
had to pass through the living room to get to the kitchen.
If I dared go out—it might stop. Sometimes my mother
would come into my room sweaty and scared and sleep with me.
And we slept. Months might have passed between beatings,
but the threat was—always—there.

So, I'd get up to piss a lot and stay up and go out and
come back and do what my mother told me to do and years
passed and I kept an eye out and I went out to look at the
girls who loved me but I had no good clue about and while
I was out—he stabbed her dead—and she was gone, and he
was gone straight to jail—and my sister and I now had to
go live with our maternal grandparents and they were old
and infirm and I kept an eye out for them and—it started—
the most ordinary thing—a short passage from a book—
over and over in my head increasingly and replaced by another
series of numbers increasingly I was crazy—of course—
look who my father was. And liquor made me feel better and
liquor and pills made it better to feel nothing and I felt
nothing when I OD'ed at 16, and, it *was* better. I should know.

8

the sweetest dream

climaxed in
iris--
we slept,
I dreamt:

                    candy colored
              baby birds--

                    afloat

         in flight--

              snowflakes
      of song--

              like

              notes of
              lovelight--

like--
looking up
at a mobile

9

These Words Are of No Help to Holly

At 51, Holly is the oldest resident at the Bronx
homeless shelter for women. Her barn owl face—features
large circular glasses in a brown plastic frame, resting
—low—on the bridge of her nose. Flabby but healthy—
with grayish-brown hair—she is the only white resident.

Tomorrow will be Christmas. Her first in 12 years without
Pumpkin and Rhett—her two mixed-bred dogs. She used to
celebrate Christmas with them, in her tiny Washington
Heights apartment that the three of them shared.
At the foot of the small fresh tree would be three care-
fully wrapped gifts. Every year, the dogs would knock
the tree down, and Holly'd go through the motions of
scolding them—inwardly, delighting in their traditional
mischief.

Within the past year both dogs died. Alone—she'd sleep
most all the time. The temp-agency stopped calling altogether.
She lost her tiny apartment. Under her bed at the shelter
—and always—within arms reach, is a 4 ounce Maxwell House
instant coffee jar. The red plastic lid—of which—has
been twisted shut tight. It contains the ashes of her dogs.
It is a small glass jar—with a red label.

10

On Sammy Off

the Background

Some people have no sense of time. Such a person
was Sammy Klazowitz. He was—always—late. That's if,
he showed up at all. As a result of this personality
trait—at around 13—he became known in our Bronx
neighborhood, as—"Sammy Off," or, simply—"Off."
Years later, a local drug-dealer theorized that a piece
of Sammy's brain had to be missing. But, I knew better.
His brain was cool. He just didn't give a fuck about
what time it was. Never did. Whatever he was doing—
smoking weed, scheming, handicapping the ponies, or
sleeping—he'd be totally into it. Nothing else mattered.
His existence transcended the ordinariness of time. He
had innate intelligence and a good heart. And, an inabil-
ity to do an—honest—days work. It was impossible for
him. More on that later. First. The first time I met him—

I was seated toward the front of the classroom in
seventh grade, on the first day of the 1967 school year,
as the teacher—Mr. Stevelman—sternly addressed us
hushed students. He was feeling us out—and we were feel-
ing him out. From the back of the class I hear—HA!
                                        HA!!
                          HA!
3 loud unrestrained mono-syllabic blasts of laughter—
the second the loudest. I turn around—it was this kid
Sammy Klazowitz. Laughing, openly, in the teacher's
face—over who knows what. He was told to shut up—and
2 laugh blasts later—he did. After I got to know Sammy
I came to realize that he wasn't trying to show the

11

teacher up. He just laughed —heartily— whenever—the fuck—he found something funny, and didn't—care to— know better.

Long as I knew him—the fifteen years to follow— this did not change. Nor, did any of the afore-mentioned features of his personality—ever change. This combination of qualities propelled him to legendary exploits. As these exploits mounted—his name further evolved and split off into the more formal—"the Officer." "The Officer," could be used interchangeably with "Off," or "Sammy Off," depending on one's arbitrary impulse, at any moment—in time.

the Root of Pathology

Six-two and about 200 lbs. the Officer was an imposing guy. He had blue eyes and curly, dirty blonde hair. But, his head was too small for his body, his complexion sallow, and his hips too wide for his shoulders. Since, his conviction the year before, on a felony—to which he pleaded guilty and got 5 years probation—he —seemed— much older. Although, I couldn't put my finger on—what it was about him—that changed. Maybe, I changed. He loved a buck. That could *never* change. He *had to* have it. Had to have it for: gambling, drugs, gas and girls. But, he did not like work. When it came to making a buck he *had to* detour at the law, or—break it.

So, he and I are sitting on the dirty, green carpeted floor, in his room—upstairs—in his parent's very modest Bronx home. A home he had yet to move from. Sitting around smoking pot and Marlboros, watching the Knicks play the 76ers, on channel 9—in 1977. We needed Knicks. I was down for 50 bucks. Phoned it into a bookie. Sammy Off's credit was no good—anywhere. But, since he made big punches—500 bucks a pop—one bookie, hungry for Off's

12

action, would dispatch one of his, long-ago broken losers, as a footman, to meet Off and get cash—up front. I was already high on seconal. We took hits of his mediocre coke intermittently. The game was tight and the dark smoky room our clearly defined world. We needed Knicks—no knock—the door swings open—

—a bare flabby arm of a woman—banana—held in hand
—is all that enters—

—a bare flabby arm of a woman—banana—held in hand—

"Sammy, nem* a banana."

The voice—his Polish Jewish mother, presenting her Samala—
a *perfect* yellow banana!

the Deeds

The window in the men's room at the Howard Johnson —across from the Bronx Zoo on Southern Boulevard—could be slid up no more than a foot. So, in order for Off to get each 5 gallon cardboard cylinder, containing ice cream—out, through that ground floor window he had to position them horizontally—before—dropping them into the back alley. Where, he'd go collect them, after, punching out on Sundays, when his shift—bussing tables—was done for the day. Off would then carry the ice cold containers—a couple blocks—to a local luncheonette, where, they were very happy to get Howard Johnson ice cream—real cheap.

The job at Howard Johnson, also, required him to fill-in, as cashier. Off mastered the cash register, and the opportunities it afforded him—to steal, real quick.

---

*nem—(Yiddish) take

13

The cash register became his "piano," and he—a virtuoso.
It was a talent that served him well, in all future em-
ployment, where, he was called upon, to cashier.

That was Sammy Off's first job—after turning 16—
and, getting his working papers. He had no vices to
support—yet. Nor, did he lack for anything at home.
Off figured—"everybody steals," and "fuck those Jew-
haters anyway." Two elements which—in combination with
one another, produce—one—powerfully compounded
—solid—position.

x x x x x x x x

Off had—only—a learners permit to drive when
the tall 17 year old—somehow—managed to get hired
—as deliveryman—for Blue Star Kosher Butchers. He was
to drive their van—delivering orders of meat to cust-
omers, and collecting payment, for these meats. He did.
He also smuggled meat out of the store and sold it. And,
regularly fleeced Blue Star of cash—sharply maneuver-
ing, as handler of—their cash. He figured, "fuck those
cheap Jews." At night he'd steal the van and shoot up to
Yonkers Raceway. He was hooked on horses. Smoked a loose
one and shot his nuts betting ponies.

As with—every—job he—ever—had, after a few
months—he was fired. Even when Sammy Off had a real
good thing—his lateness—was certain. As certain, as
the sunrise. At 18, he got his driver's license. By 19,
he was blacklisted by—every—yellow cab company in
Manhattan. He'd show-up late—work a couple hours—
take the cab to the track—get "robbed," and return the
cab—emptyhanded. Sometimes, right before returning the
cab—he'd report the "robbery" to the local police pre-
cinct—where—he, "got robbed."

14

A couple years later Off bought a used two-door,
red, black-top, fast-back Cutlass. A sharp car—never—
to be washed again. We could now—shoot—to Roosevelt
Raceway, out on Long Island. Crossing the Whitestone
Bridge—we'd look for an automated tollbooth, where,
the wooden arm, that—must—be in the—up—position,
in order to drive on through, was, in the—up—position,
and—not—operating, but, the lane—not—blocked off.
Conditioned drivers would stop their cars by the metal
basket and mindlessly drop their coins into it. We'd go
right through—never—paying. Sammy Off spotted this
—instantly—for the set-up that it was. Unaudited
monies collected, to be split-up among "the boys" work-
ing that shift.

Sometimes—coming back—if no toll was set-up for
"the boys," the Officer would drive right through a manned
booth—slapping his empty hand hard against the toll
collector's open palm—
HA!
   HA!!
HA!
Done—and never caught. After we won—at the track—
or lost.

x x x x x x x x

Never, a lucky gambler, he was—a good handicapper.
And, for a week or two—could get very hot. During these
scientifically (as opposed to luck) fueled hot streaks,
I—only—had to reach into my pocket—to cover, my own
bets. Diner costs, track admissions and programs, bar
tabs, and pot—he covered. But, money in his pocket,
did—not—mean—payment—for his creditors. Unless,
he was confronted with imminent physical danger, by
capable bone-breakers, he wasn't paying—anyone.

15

One—winning—night, we're up in the clubhouse—
at Yonkers Raceway, and, on this—Saturday—night,
even the clubhouse is packed. We're standing under-
neath one of the televised tote boards—smoking,
handicapping, and occasionally looking up—at the
televised tote board, when—a cologne necked muscle
soaked enforcer—spots the Officer, for someone who
—he believes—has reneged on a couple hundred—owed—
the storefront bookie joint—where, the enforcer, was
one of several clerks. He believed right.

He comes over to where we're standing, "I know you,"
he accusingly tells the Officer—as though the Officer
was disguised as a tea kettle—but, couldn't fool him—
his left index finger in Off's chest. "WHAT'RE—YOU—
SOME KIND OF HOMO?" the Officer shouts into his face—and
the eyes of the crowd of gamblers—some with girlfriends—
fix upon a—now—confused and self-conscious, cologne
necked muscle soaked enforcer—who slinks away shaking
his head left to right to left...

The unshakable Officer sensed some uncertainty, and,
so—the cologne necked muscle soaked enforcer was victim-
ized, by—the mastermind of reversism. He was not the
first such victim, nor, would he be the last.

× × × × × × × ×

I unloaded the last—of the truckload—of large
cartons—that had previously been packed by Off with
100 small boxes of Kotex sanitary napkins per carton—
off, of Off's rented truck. The owner of the south Bronx
drug store—in front of which—we were double-parked,
was now doing a quick count of them, as Off hovered over
his back—bombing the bald top of the old druggist's
radish-like head with bluish cigarette smoke exhalations.
That, each small sample box had imprinted on it—sample
not for sale—mattered not, to this owner of drug stores.

16

Grinning a self-congratulatory grin, he handed the Officer crisp cash—and we were gone.

This caper was made possible, when a prominent marketing firm hired the Officer to manage a short term project for them. He, was to, manage the distribution of small sample boxes of Kotex sanitary napkins, throughout, a slice of Westchester. They never bothered to check Off's —fraudulent—resume. He—being naturally delusional— believed it. Why shouldn't they?

Not only were no samples distributed to the public, but, also—the entire amount allocated for payroll, was paid to—himself, under several aliases—and me. He was a generous guy. I got several pay checks for doing nothing, and I didn't even have to kickback. Over the next couple of days—most—all the money made from the Kotex sample box sale, was "donated," to the track.

x x x x x x x x

No regulars at the track are winners. None. Losers all. The "game" grinds you into dust. With only loose change left between the two of us, after, another losing night—and, the fuel indicator well below E—we were feeling very lucky—just—to make it back. Suddenly— a big black Buick Wildcat cuts us off—screeching smokily— to a stop—causing the Officer to slam the brakes on the Cutlass—bringing us to a screeching stop. The big black Wildcat is known to us.

A loose-built long haired giant emerges—in sections— from the driver's side. A guy—over—a foot shorter muscular and bald—has jumped out the other side. The big guy is the Big Bluff, and—the other—his right hand— Mahatmo. The Big Bluff—named in dishonour of his crappy poker game. And, Mahatmo—for his phony machismo and overall crappiness. Tight-fisted glowers pasted—the duo

17

approaches. We've remained seated as they position them-
selves—one—at each of our doors. The Big Bluff—
the loose-built long-haired giant by Off's door, and,
his boy—the muscular short and bald jazz-commando
—Mahatmo—by mine.

"You got till Thursday to pay up," is the Big Bluff's
ultimatum to the Officer—an ultimatum issued by the
deep-toking marijuana marathoner through orthodontically
adjusted horsey choppers
HA!
      HA!!
HA!
The Officer laughs right in his face. Muttering—bloody
Thursday threats—the Big Bluff and Mahatmo hop back
into the Wildcat, and tear off under the el. Apparently,
Sammy Off buying the Big Bluff all the cereal he could
eat, and then turning him on to super potent sweet black
opiated hash panacea—after, the Bluff's parents threw
their son out of the house last year—didn't count for
much, anymore—to the towering—former—poker player
—forever—pot glutton—
HA!
      HA!!
HA!
I couldn't stop laughing either.

                    x x x x x x x x

The Officer took a couple of civil service tests—
and scored on top. Presented well at the interview, and
was hired—by the New York State Dept. of Taxation and
Finance, as—a tax-compliance agent. There couldn't
have been much of a background check done on him. If
there was, they would have discovered—several—misdem-
eanor convictions. Just one month prior, he was arrested
when police raided an abandoned Harlem building—where,
he was one of 87 men arrested—betting on live dog-fights.

18

As a tax-compliance agent, the 23 year old Sammy Off,
was to visit businesses that were tax delinquent, and
effect collection. He had the power to: seize bank
accounts, and shut-down businesses. On the days he was
required to work—in—the office, he'd show-up late.
As a result, he became the first and only agent—ever—
to have to punch-in, on the clock. This, had no effect
on his lateness.

However, when he was out in the field, and—actually—
worked—this bettor of horses, ballgames, and dogs—
would astound his supervisor, with superior productivity.
This, in spite of the fact that much of the time he was
supposed to be—out in the field—working, he'd be
home—asleep. He had added a new quinella to his reper-
toire—cocaine and girls. Deeply seasoned in deceit—
he was shy, and green—when it came to girls. He had yet
to learn that girls did not have to be an expense. Gamb-
ling, drugs, and girls: a breakneck action box for—
the Officer.

Lots of cash was needed, for him—to carry on. He
began shaking-down tax debtors. Some, who knew they were
being shook-down. Others, who knew they were being shook-
down—but, didn't want to know. And, one who didn't even
know he was being shook-down. In every case—cash—to
the Officer, was cheaper than—checks—to the govern-
ment. And, the Officer mastered the art of the shake-down.
However, his breakneck action box proved to be a natural
disaster so ravenous, it overwhelmed—even—his artistry.
He ended up copping a plea to a felony—and was sentenced
to 5 years probation, and a $5,000. fine.

He spent the next several months amassing the cash—
by dealing large amounts of quaaludes, he'd acquire—
from an acquaintance, who was a pharmacist. The pharmacist
was under pressure: to support his wife and two children,
in a comfortable lifestyle. The Officer was under pressure

19

to: make payments on the fine, gamble, and get high. He
did—however—get himself a couple—low maintenance—
girlfriends.

Epilogue

That was then. Today, the 43 year old—Officer—
lives in Florida, with his wife—Rhonda, and their two
children. They've been married for over 15 years. The
marriage has had some rocky spots, but they've always
stayed together. He's toned down his gambling, and
—only—smokes pot. Their two children: a girl of 13—
Cara, and, a boy of 10—Larry, are adorable, and appear
to be doing well. Although, some say—that the Officer
puts undue pressure on skilled little Larry—drilling—
into the psyche of his young son, Off's own—living—
adolescent Yankee fantasy. His wife—Rhonda—runs her
own small business—a local day-care center. Assisted
by her staff—of one—she handles everything. Her work
day is long, and exhausting.

The Officer, works part-time—but earns more. He
sells ad-space in community-watch newspapers, that he
publishes. This is his fifth year in this business. His,
is a one man operation. He is very adept at enabling
potential customers to exhibit their civic responsi-
bility—by kicking-in to support their community-watch
paper. His unflappability, resolve, and resourcefulness
combine to make his pitch a kind of—customized voodoo.
His success rate selling space to immigrant owners of
retail establishments is exceptionally good. He regularly
acquires new accounts, and, although—none—of his cus-
tomers have ever seen the ads they've paid for—many,
continue to advertise regularly. Actually, *no one* has
ever seen—any—of the papers he publishes. Not even
him.

20

50

U.S.A. FIVE DOLLARS

Bones & Jokes

NYQ Books, 2009

Poems

These Words Are of No Help to Holly

At 51, Holly is the oldest resident at the Bronx
homeless shelter for women. Her barn owl face—features
large circular glasses in a brown plastic frame, resting
—low—on the bridge of her nose. Flabby but healthy—
with grayish-brown hair—she is the only white resident.

Tomorrow will be Christmas. Her first in 12 years without
Pumpkin and Rhett—her two mixed-breed dogs. She used to
celebrate Christmas with them, in her tiny Washington
Heights apartment that the three of them shared.
At the foot of the small fresh tree would be three care-
fully wrapped gifts. Every year, the dogs would knock
the tree down, and Holly'd go through the motions of
scolding them—inwardly, delighting in their traditional
mischief.

Within the past year both dogs died. Alone—she'd sleep
most all the time. The temp-agency stopped calling altogether.
She lost her tiny apartment. Under her bed at the shelter
—and always—within arms reach, is a 4 ounce Maxwell House
instant coffee jar. The red plastic lid—of which—has
been twisted shut tight. It contains the ashes of her dogs.
It is a small glass jar—with a red label.

Son of Sam

Clapping, he'd look around; at the other boys on
his side of the volleyball court who were clapping.
When they stopped, he stopped.

Burly, friendless, and blank—

Berkowitz. In black dress socks, gym shorts, and
sneakers. Back in high school gym class.

Spent a couple years as a peacetime soldier, and moved
on to become a nighttime postal worker; before he got
busted for being—

Son of Sam. Girl hunter who'd thunder them bloody with
his 44. A self-described, "chubby behemoth." Who heard
his killing orders in the—

Barking. Out his window. In the alley. Sam Carr's dog—
BARKING BARKING BARKING BARKING—

Berkowitz. Showed you. Chose to. Show you.
KILLING KILLING KILLING KILLING—

BREATH-ING!

Regina Einhorn

(written after my cancer diagnosis, 11/2/06)

What planet she's
dropped from,
nobody knows.

She hunts alone.

Coolly cruising
Rochambeau Avenue:
legs and
more legs, casual hips,
jagged shag, pillow lips,
and a mannish
two finger pinch
on her Parliament.

17, and
she out-Klutes
Jane Fonda.

A mixed pack
of cocksure
Bib & Sam's candy
store hanging deep-
toking James Dean-
afflicted egomaniacs
flex their blue jean
buttocks, but she
somehow plucks me.

Makes a man feel—
so proud.

Chats Fender
Stratocaster and
Gibson SG.
Tells me to read
Narcissus and Goldmund.
And that she's tight with
Humble Pie.

Seeks:
"A real good-looking
guy with sensitive eyes,
to hang with locally."

Last night I was too
stoned to crawl out
of a two-feet-deep
Bronx Park East ditch.

Tonight,
amid the brush, beneath
the silver carving moon,
it's me and blue-denim
miniskirt clad, red
lipstick adorned, rooted
Regina.

"I feel *very* submissive,"
she says, nonchalantly.

"Hummana, hummana, hummana…"
I am Ralph Kramden.
And hear the soft, low,
surging trill of a small
(voyeuristic?) owl, before
I collapse inwardly.

*****

Across a great green lawn,
hand in hand, walks Regina,
with another man.

And I wonder,
where in this melted pot
Bronx Gehenna did that
breezy babe find an All-
American, long-blond-
haired, hippie stud named—
Atticus Rasper?

That was three-quarters
of a lifetime ago.
Since then,

I've survived:
A bat attack,
"Hey Jude," and
Thorazine.

Have screwed
seven beauties,
read the Bible,
kicked Big Brother
in the balls, and
learned to love.

But if that unfinished
Regina business
haunts me still—

I need to get cancer.

what goes down must come up

buried by the buried boy,
beneath the mudslide of miles
of noise,

climbs a punctured heart that will
not die, and when it does reach
the top,

before it topples back,
blood leaks warmly out my eyes—

never am I more alive—

Third Floor

Our next door neighbor was a tall young lady. Denberg was the name on her door. She was raising a little girl and boy alone. Don't know how I knew her first name was Judy. Her boy was nine. Two years younger than me. His name was Jody. An older man moved in with them. The name on the door then read Colello/Denberg. He was a cheap-looking cocka-doodle-doo in a three-quarter black leather coat. Like my father. Across from us lived a well-groomed kid in his late teens with good posture who wore burgundy penny loafers. I thought he might have a classy accent, but he never said boo. I don't recall ever seeing his parents, but was sure the neatly twined stack of books which would sometimes appear by the incinerator chute had belonged to them. Four more doors. In the far corner was a red-headed divorcee and her two kids. Her loner son Steven Stoltz was my age. He was good with dogs and roamed the streets and alleys surrounded by mangy strays. One night his shapely older sister Carol was sitting on our front stoop, her transistor radio blasting something new, "All Day and All of the Night," by The Kinks. The song was exciting. And so was she. Three apartments housed lone old ladies. Two of whom were no longer capable of carrying their chairs downstairs to sit in front of the building. One could, but never did. Her name was Ceil. She knew how to talk to people. And liked my mother. More than once, she would knock on our door and ask, *What's wrong in there?*

A Better Man

She fought them off. Starch-collared, anything-for-
another-lousy-buck jackals, who hungered to disfigure
majestic Grand Central Station. So I'm glad they
renamed The Central Park Reservoir for Jackie O.

On a bench, by that hundred-plus acre body of water,
I soak up some early spring sun. Daydream revelation
and baseball. A merry-go-round of joggers in all shapes
and sizes doggedly run the track which surrounds
the water. A gangly, shaggy-haired kid seats himself
on the track, leisurely leaning against the ornamental
cast-iron fence which separates it from the water.
Hooked up to his iPod, he rolls a smoke. Paperback
in lap. Girlfriend to his left. She's a dark-eyed beauty.
A ballerina. Or a dream. Maybe he's listening to alter-
native rock, maybe Anarchy R Us, while catching up
on some required reading. Maybe he needs all that
simultaneous stimulation because he's a genius. More
likely, he's Holden Caulfield lolling in the luxury of
teenage angst. He absently blows gray bursts of smoke
toward the passing joggers. Maybe the joggers deserve
to be smoked. But why, I wonder, doesn't one kick
the smoke from the self-absorbed twit's hand? And
wonder on…when I hear, "I'm Dan Ingram and I'm
a *better* man than you." Turn to face a crusty old
stranger sitting on the other end of the bench, sporting
a "Korean War Veteran" cap and a happy-drunk grin.
Again he says, "I'm Dan Ingram and I'm a *better* man
than you." "Yeah," I say. "You are a *better* man than me."
Nod toward the kid and add, "But I'm a *better* man than
him." Dan Ingram points at the kid and says, "Him?"
"Yeah," I say. "*Him.* How come it doesn't occur to
him that blowing smoke into gasping joggers' faces
is wrong?" "Simple," says Dan Ingram. "He never got
his ass kicked. Never." And I know he's right. And know
I'm right when I say, "And you know, the amazing thing
is he may never. Ever."

CHINATOWN

Snapping pictures of adulterers in the act is an honest living.
A fine living for fast on his feet, tailored, tough guy,
P.I. Jake Gittes. Smoke. Drink. Joke. And smile, smile, smile
your I'm-in-love-with-myself-so-you-should-be-too smile.
Forget about the girl you couldn't save in Chinatown.

High-class alabaster blonde mindfucker Mrs. Mulwray,
Ida whatever, Walt Disney's mouse...Does it really matter
who hired you to snap shots of Mr. Mulwray with his mistress?
You got paid. It's 30s boomtown L.A.
Forget about the girl you couldn't save in Chinatown.

Why take on venerated old tycoon Noah Cross?
A whale of a man. Creator of his own cash ocean.
That a man is old and made of money does not mean
he no longer needs more—
What are you, Jake, some kind of Red?

Why take on the L. A. Dept. of Water and Power?
The puny big-nosed refugee who blithely switchblade-sliced
your trespassing nose into bloody pulp with a single stroke,
he knows how life plays out in this world of ours.
Forget about the girl you couldn't save in Chinatown.

What's it to you if Noah Cross owns the water supply?

What's it to you if Noah Cross rapes the ghostly 13-year-old
girl he sired raping his daughter, the recently widowed
Mrs. Mulwray?

Mrs. Mulwray is dead. Finely-chiseled face lawfully blown off.

Old Noah Cross. Gnarly and huge. A leafless tree.
Stiff boughs hang tangled over ghostly girl-child shoulders,
clutching her mute open mouth and a teensy naked knee.
Bone-girl. From behind. Reared into his rude trunk.

Cops saw. But only you could taste her sour yellow terror.

Haircut

The traditional peppermint twist pole,
and—$10.00 a cut, plus tip—price,
sold me on Isaac's Best Haircuts Barbershop.

Bolodenka, a gentleman from Uzbekistan,
who spoke little English, did an OK job for me.

Before every haircut I'd say, "Not too short."

After every haircut he'd say, "See you next month."

And so it was, with each month torn from my
2003 Fleet Bank Desk Calendar,
for over a year.

One afternoon—
Comb and scissors clipping my hair in tandem,
he paused *twice* to gaze across the room—
TV game show action.

Bolo, baby,
Zen Buddhists say:
When I eat, I eat.
When I sleep, I sleep.

I say:
When you cut my hair, you cut my hair—
No American-style multi-tasking bullshit.

But, instead, I remained silent.
No need to waste energy.
Fuck Bolodenka!

=

The traditional peppermint twist pole,
and—$12.00 a cut, plus tip—price,
sold me on Executive Barbershop.

Yakov, a gentleman from Russia,
who spoke little English, did an OK job for me.

Before every haircut I'd say, "Not too short."

After every haircut he'd try to sell me conditioner.

And so it was, with each month torn from my
2004 Fleet Bank Desk Calendar,
for over a year.

One afternoon—
Comb and scissors clipping my hair in tandem,
Three muffled musical notes buzzed into our air—
He paused, reached for the cell phone,
and tucked it between his left shoulder and ear.
Yammering Russian and clipping my hair.

Yakov, baby,
Zen Buddhists say:
When I eat, I eat.
When I sleep, I sleep.

I say:
When you cut my hair, you cut my hair—
No American-style multi-tasking bullshit.

But, instead, I remained silent.
No need to waste energy.
Fuck Yakov!

=

Up in the Bronx,
there was Foo's Gift Shop, on Belmont.
Mr. Foo sold bags and backpacks,
porcelain elephant plant stands,
and replaced watch batteries.

In back, was a metal folding chair.
On which, I sat. Relaxed—

As a dark-eyed,
orange butterfly, fluttered above me.
Snipping a song—for $8.00 flat.

GRACE

I liked you and your
unsmiling, ghetto bred,
Hungarian father
a lot.

His huge head of black curls,
leaden handshake, retiring dark
eyes, and Popeye forearms.

That he seemed partial to
short sleeves, unashamed
of his numerical, blurry, blue
Auschwitz tattoo.

And you, Grace,
a studious cherry rice pudding,
behind Coke bottle granny glasses,
hopeful, oceanic gray eyes—

Told me your father firmly replied
no thanks, he'd rather stay home and
rest than accept your offer to treat
him to *Fiddler on the Roof* for his
birthday.

You suspected he really
did not know
the true date of his birth.

He told you his full-bearded, orthodox
father had toiled as a chairmender,
and he himself pressed garments at the
dry cleaning plant.
But you…

The way he watched out for you
was right.

Silently,
sizing me up as I played it cool
on Kuklemonga Street.

Staring back, I noticed that his tattoo
started with a triangle.

I hope
he survived to see his baby Grace
become a scholar and a mother,
moving from the Bronx to Wisconsin
and on to Haifa.

And know you burn too,
knowing there's a viral-eyed,
squeaky Ahmadinejad who
says your father never existed.

19 Actions More Practical than Writing this Poem

Assaulting the wall with my head. Switching to a raw food diet.
Curing cat co-dependency. Channeling Elvis. Blaming the messenger.
Playing computer solitaire. Playing lotto. Playing the kazoo.
Petitioning the lord with prayer. Massaging my prostate.
Assaulting the wall with *your* head. Reading Thackeray's Vanity Fair.
Taking up golf. Dancing the Funky Chicken. Shaving my chest.
Casting a vote for American Idol. Collecting Nazi war memorabilia.
Shouting Bama Lama, Bama Loo. Netting butterflies. Collecting dust.

TOMMY BOLAN

The raggy, rage-filled voice of my father spasmed noise
to match the noise made, as he harshly shoved kitchen
furniture on the linoleum floor—

      to get to mom?

I—was a little kid, in the darkness of my bed—her cries
were muffled—the door stayed closed, I couldn't sleep—

      was he hitting her?

My little sister slept in the other bed. It was the only
bedroom of the 3 room apartment. On the other side of the
shut door was a small foyer. To the left was the bathroom.
On the right was the doorless arched entrance to the living
room—where our parents would sleep on the sofa bed. You
had to pass through the living room to get to the kitchen.
If I dared go out—it might stop. Sometimes my mother
would come into my room sweaty and scared and sleep with me.
And we slept. Months might have passed between beatings,
but the threat was—always—there.

So, I'd get up to piss a lot and stay up and go out and
come back and do what my mother told me to do and years
passed and I kept an eye out and I went out to look at the
girls who loved me but I had no good clue about and while
I was out—he stabbed her dead—and she was gone, and he
was gone straight to jail—and my sister and I now had to
go live with our maternal grandparents and they were old
and infirm and I kept an eye out for them and—it started—
the most ordinary thing—a short passage from a book—
over and over in my head increasingly and replaced by another
series of numbers increasingly I was crazy—of course—
look who my father was. And liquor made me feel better and
liquor and pills made it better to feel nothing and I felt
nothing when I OD'ed at 16, and it *was* better. I should know.

THE VOLUNTEER

Steaming in the August stench of Times Square,
my co-worker and I scooted and sidled through
the stylish rush hour roil of office workers,
when she turned to me and, through whiter than
white teeth, said:

"I believe in giving something back, so I'm on
my way to St. Ignatius's Church. Tonight is my
night to serve supper to the homeless."

"That's kind of you," I said.

"What about you?" she asked.
"What do you do?"

"I never got anything,
so I've got nothing to give back."

Unfazed, she turned away.
We walked on, side by side.

Amid the swarming sidewalk stood a copper-
colored, short and sturdy, gray-braided woman
wearing a sandwich board sign: *Men's Suits—
Blowout Sale!*

She held out flyers for passersby. As though
she were a fire hydrant, all passed her by.
I stepped over to her. Face glistened metallic
sweat. Took a flyer and said, "Thank you."

For This, You Motherfuckers Will Not Be Getting 70 Virgins

There, on the wailing wall at Grand Central:

MISSING
since 9-11

Smile of a birthday boy—

A brown Buddha this young man Clyde Bevins Junior,

The kind of guy who would never abandon his old mama
to a nursing home,

A messenger planning to study architecture—

"Not a bad bone in his body," said a Stork Messenger
Service co-worker, of his fellow Mets fan.

A man born to be the good father!

"EVERY MORNING I SEE YOU SMILING, I MISS YOU,
WE NEVER MET."

On a card taped next to his picture,
anonymously—

DAMON'S WAY

1 operable
pay phone in this
uptown burned
down 'hood and
this large shoul-
dered crack dealer is
dominating it.
his hooded lookout
hangs loose and their un-
leashed pit bull stays:
ugly. waiting for
the phone,

damon, is as sig-
nificant to the
ambitious dealer
—as say—that
passing stray, white,
black-pawed cat.

damon
takes a quick
last glance at the
grinning dealer and
starts turning, to split
—NOW—

that cat—is
—CRUNCHED—instantly:
broken, muted, and
limp—in the indust-
rial locked jaws
of the bucket head-
ed 50 lb. pit,
the pit, collared
has—now—been
suspended

in air "the cat
started it!" blurts
the dealer, phone-
less, as he and his
lookout incred-
ulously witness

damon dangling their
gurgling cat crunching
pit in mid-air,
twisting

its collar
violently
to cut the pit's
air. looking, arms
length from his
taut bruce lee bo-
dy damon wonders—
when did I grab this
killer pit?
60

seconds later the
choked pit un-
locks and drops the
broken backed collapsed
but not very
bloody barely breath-
ing cat, to the

pavement, and
damon tosses the
whimpering
pit to the pave-
ment, and man

nor dog did
shit, as damon laid
the small mass of cat
into the flat back
of his double-parked
2-door rusting
gray toyota hatch-
back starlet, and

ran many lights
on the way to the
24 hours a
day emergency
drop-off at the

ASPCA
on 1st avenue
by 89th street,
and in his
heart he
knew

the cat had not
many breaths left,
and when they got there—
he saw, that the bro-
ken backed collapsed cat
had belly

crawled up, and was
curled beside
him, and damon was
moved to let the cat
die right there,
with dignity—
by his side, but
instead,

opted to do
his "duty,"
to take the cat
inside, where,
maybe—they could op-
erate, and the cat—
survive. the dying
cat

strengthless struggled
against damon's
arms, struggled
to stay, in—
the car. in the A
SPCA

a volun-
teer took the broken
backed collapsed cat from
damon's arms and
laid it into a
too small cage,
even if the cat

—could've—stood
it wouldn't have been
able to in that
too small cage,
and as the volun-

teer whisked the
cat to the back
room damon wit-
nessed the cat quake,
and as damon left,
he crumblestuffed the
receipt he'd gotten
for the cat into
the left pocket of
his jeans, where he kept
—only—his keys, on
a ring, and half

an hour
later he called
and was told the
cat quaked
20 minutes
straight and
died, and damon
got

down, on himself—
for not letting
the cat die, with
dignity—
by his side, and
as damon wiped vo-
mitbloodshit from the
black vinyl flat back
of his hatchback

thunder-
ous self-hatred wreaked
merciless havoc.

this last fact is
one key in un-
derstanding damon's
impulsive act, of

homeric courage—
bare handedly
rescuing the cat
—out—the deathlock
jaws of the infer-
nal bucket-headed
beast, something

you, nor anyone
you've ever met—
would, or could—
do.

HURLY-BURLY BUROO

—A concoction created to ward off a five-time draft deferred, shotgun toting, septuagenarian reptile clad in an orange vest.

asshole of a tarantula
low john root
10 yenta tongues
wattle of a rooster
essence of a rose
clit ring of a whore
wahoo root bark
sumac berries
Ed Bradley's earring
underbelly of a wild boar
ingrown toenail of a centenarian
90 milligrams methadone
eyeball of a Cyclops
Mr. Potato Head
tonsils of Deep Throat
a partridge and a pear tree
foreskin of an elephant
heart of a flea
wallet of a schnorr
broom straws
1 Big Mac
2 hunchbacks
hot licks and deer ticks
whiskers of a hipster
left testicle of a sex addict
entrails of a sewer rat
violet leaf
liver of a sot
a purring furry cat

12 pints blood /
from any billionaire real estate developer
sprinkle MSG
and

boil it all in a pot.

Boychick Exquisite

Looking up from my crib,
I saw a small stuffed tiger
being handed down to me.
Somehow—
I knew it belonged to me.

Maybe,
I had played with it before.
I don't remember.

Firstborn,
and,
a boy child:
I struck grandma's hand with
my toy guitar,
my dark hair turned blond,
the blow broke her finger,
my mother let my loose curls
grow long I
looked like a girl—
I don't remember.

Grandma would show-off her
crooked finger to me.

I remember—
calling for my mother,
while running to the toilet—
and waiting for her—
jumping around,
and waiting.
A boychick exquisite—
I had blessed her.

HEARTS TO CLUBS

"I'm out,"

says Milt, the father of our host, as he folds his cards. Bloated and wasted, in his fifties, he's about thirty years older than me and the three other players seated around the table. He turns to his son who's still in. He tells him:

"Ya dunno watda fuck ya doin' an' it's fuckin' ME up."

His son doesn't even look at him. He's locked in on the pot. Milt splashes some cologne on his scalp and combs his three hairs straight back. Broke. He rises. And heads to the toilet.

Seven card poker. In the single-room Bronx basement apartment. On the bicentennial.

Campbell deals the final round—down. Clockwise, to those players still in the pot: our host, Philip, me, and himself. Our host pulls his cards slow and opens with a buck bet. Looks left at who's next—and says to him:

"It's to you Philip FuckinRetard."

Philip laughs nervously. He babbles. Campbell yells at him:

"Shutdafuckup!"

He does—but not before he ups the bet another buck. It's to me—there's about forty bucks in the pot. I need to squeeze a heart for a flush—any heart—I need to squeeze a heart—a heart to the hearts—a heart to the hearts— a heart—

"Ya inna out?"
—Clubs—

TARANTULA DANCE

He walks on water,
has 8 eyes,
8 relentless long legs,
1" fangs,

and forges over
miles of jungle land,

following her wind-
blown mating scent
to its source—

the silk of her burrow.

There,
his hairy black ball
body vibrates
a trilling invitation
while front legs stamp
a rhythmic shiver
of need...

She emerges—
a brown mirror image
of him.

Not immune
to his own poison,
he approaches hot
with cold caution.

She has been known
 to change her mind—

might kill and eat him.

He holds her.
She holds him.

Gently, he taps her—
ta-ta-ta-ta-taps…

Sixteen intertwined
spindly legs sway this
way and that—
ta-ta-ta-ta-taps…

Sixty plus minutes,
till she's slack in a trance.

Seed planted…
he flees for his life.

Myles Spenser

Passed out. Died. Dope OD. Twenty-three. My powerful, round body was carried out of the shooting gallery into the South Bronx sunlight, laid out by the front stoop and abandoned. One block from where I grew up.

The old man loved dope. After decades of dope, he settled for methadone, a part-time gig driving a limo, and J&B Whisky. The old lady yelled at the walls. She was heavy into bingo. I got a younger brother, Jay. A nickel-and-dime methadone addict. I tried to throw him out a window for…I forget what. Don't remember ever caring about any of them.

The year I turned 23, moved to a better neighborhood. There, I met Baker. Dug him. Handed him a bag of pot and told him to take as much as he wanted. Told him how the hit-and-run left me with a steel-pin in my hip and glass eye. And if anyone ever bothered him, to let me know—because I don't expect to make 25.

I fucked-up a huge Fordham U. football player outside a nightclub. I fucked-up a pimp, poolside, in Miami. I let Eddie Thomas get the better of me, because I liked him—and he was right.

I ate it up when Baker and the boys would go on about great I was, and loved to hear my deep, sweet voice talk them up.

The boys shot dope. I dove in. I ripped-off a dealer. Pulled him right out from behind the wheel of his van. We all got-off on the roof. I mugged an old man, bloodied his fine blue pinstriped Sunday suit.

I shot big hits. The day my dead body was found, I shot a lot of good-shit.

Jay Spenser

I needed that token clerk job. So, I stepped up to the urinal next to where some chump was pissin'—and took it. Stuck my plastic cup under his piss—and took it. He ran out, the faggot. HA-HA! Washed my hands. My own urine was dirty, and I wouldn't have got the job. Piss I hijacked got me that job.

A piss I took a couple years before that almost got me killed. A bunch of us were up at Baker's. I was feelin' real nice on extra meth and sprayed weed. So I follow my girl, Bernice, into the bathroom where she sits on the pot to piss—and does. Stand over her, so I can piss between her legs—and do. All the time we're laughin', and a couple guys come in and watch and laugh and watch—

This flips my crazy ass-kickin' brother Myles out. He comes blowin' in from the livin' room and grabs me by my hair and throat. My dick still out—drippin'—he drags me into the livin' room. Tries to throw me out the sixth floor window. Didn't like what I was doin' with Bernice. If it was Slow Boat or Baker doin' it—guys he liked—he wouldn't have cared. Might've laughed. But it was me. It took 3 guys and a screamin' Bernice to save my life.

All that goes back…gotta be 5-6 years. Myles died—OD. Then ma dropped dead at the bingo hall—heart attack. And last year, the old man's liver finally gave. I didn't go claim his body at the city morgue. Fuck it. He was dead, and I needed cash. Cash—gonna get kicked out this rathole if I don't kick in to that junkie bitch Connie. Shit—I used to get foxy chicks. Twenty-eight come May—look like shit. A bony goat's ghost. Feel like shit. Bad as when I was flat on my back at Bronx Lebanon—starin' crazy pain at ceilin', nose broke, kickin' smack—alone. Wished I was dead. Well, I'm alone. But now I ain't on my back. I'm goin'—out her window. The sixth floor—the same floor Myles tried to throw me from. HA-HA! Only this time it's on my own. And piss—got nothin' to do with it.

The President's Daughter Caught a Big Fish in Kennebunkport

Third straight Thursday 3:00 p.m. lunch break,
at the counter of Primo's Diner, down on Broadway—

Same brunette waitress, with the odd eyes
(one fierce and blue, the other lazy, filmy-gray),
Betty Boop boobs,
and Eastern European accent.

"Hi!" I say.

"Hello," she replies.

"I'll have a tuna salad platter, coffee, and water."

Flip through the first few pages of the *Daily News*—
She returns with the coffee and water.

"I'm Ted."

"I am Petra."

"Is that Russian?"

"Polish."

"Oh, my mother was from Poland. Polish Jew.
Called me Tadeusz."

"Tadeusz, Petra...These are good names, yes?"

"Yes."

Cecil Beaton beckons for a coffee refill—
She scurries off.
Flip through the rest of the paper, sip coffee...

Petra returns with the ample tuna salad platter.
Which includes: potato salad, cucumber, tomato,
2 packets of Melba toast, coleslaw, and a hard-boiled egg,
 spread on a bed of lettuce. Sets it gently down before me.

Casting her blue eye at my *Daily News,* she asks—
"What is news?"

"The president's daughter caught a big fish in Kennebunkport."

 She laughs, throatily.

Silently, picks up a packet of my Melba toast.
Long nurturing fingers flawlessly tear open the cellophane.
She consecrates the second packet similarly. All—

For me.

And I want to say something warm—
Something wonderful—

But I've got a mouthful of potato salad—

Then she was gone.

A Lion is a Cow

Meat I ate was once a lion.
Had to be. My mother told me
it would make me strong.
Like a lion.

She'd cut it up for me, into
little pieces. I'd leave the last
piece. She'd say: the last
piece was the key.

Years later: I learned,
meat I ate was not a lion.
I was: hurtshocked.
A cow?

the sweetest dream

climaxed in
iris—
we slept,
I dreamt:

           candy colored
          baby birds—

              afloat

          in flight—

              snowflakes
                of song—

          like

          notes of
              lovelight—

         like—

looking up,
from my crib—
at a mobile—

          wide-eyed

Dealing in Prayer

(at 26)

Lift—*1—18—2—9—?? 1—18—*
this—*1—18—2—9—20—18—1—18—25*
curse—*1—18—2—??*—from me.
God—this
1—18—2—9—20—18—1—18—25
CLATTEREXACT
jack—*1—18—??*—hammer
1—18—2—9—20—18—1—18—25
Mind demolisher
And—*1—18—2—9—?? 1—18—2—9—20?*
I will never beg another favor.
1—18—2—9—20—18—1—18—25
1—18—2—9—20—18—1—18—25
1—18—2—9—20—??

Having no faith to pray:

PLEASE HEAR MY PLEAS TO DEAL!
1—18—2—9—And I will—*1—18—*
never beg—*2—9—20—18—1—18—25*
—another favor. *1—18—2—9—??*

And my upper lip swelled,

1—18—2—9—20—18—1—18—25
1—18—?? 1—18—2—9?
1—18—2—9—20—18—1—18—25

And my body stiffened,

1—18—2—9—??
1—18—2—9—20—18?

I lay listless nine days.

On the tenth day I arose
And realized, that
As I lay stricken, the curse had been
Lifted.

And I said to Him:

I have known the curse that has been
Lifted.

And I will never beg another favor.
And I will hide and not be cursed
Again.

WHITE MEN IN SANDALS

On the Fahrenheit scale the boiling point of water is 212.
On the Fahrenheit scale the all-white-men-in-Manhattan-slip-into-sandals point is 55.

In low white Cons I ran for my life real fast across Bronx concrete.
In steel-tipped black boots I stood fast and kicked shin-cracking low.
In high-gloss black police oxfords I passed as an off-duty cop.
Today, in black New Balance walking shoes, I walk Manhattan.
They have taken over.

Foul-footed exhibitionists,
unprepared for fight or flight.

Men from Idaho with enormous feet.
Men from France with itsy-bitsy feet.
Men from Long Island with filthy feet.
A John Ashbery acolyte with cloven feet.

As though there were a date with Miss Japan at stake, they patiently wait in long lines at
trendy City Bakery, breaking out the plastic to pay $12.50 per pound to lunch on slightly
above average salad bar crap from a paper plate.

Sans the support of innersoles they subway to Yankee Stadium. Taking in the art deco
Grand Concourse, which they will invade. Turning live poultry markets into vintage
clothes shops and the saint-haven botanicas into pet spas.

Deep auto exhaust inhalers, they dine at upscale sidewalk cafes, viewing scenic black
mountain ranges of rancid garbage packed 58-gallon plastic trash bags, and a parade of
shitting dogs. Why not just toss a tablecloth over the hood of a parked Buick?

Always ready to hop the jitney to Southampton.

Maybe someday, I too, will let my doggies breathe.

REDEMPTION

Don't remember any Little League team names,
not even the one I was on. Nor do I remember
the coach or manager or whatever he was called,
except that there *was* one, and his doofus son
played first base. We played at Grenadier Field.
That I'm sure of. Because I remember warming
the bench and wondering who was this Grenadier
guy? I quickly concluded he was a dead man
who had always worn a suit and tie to work.
Except for Beaver's father, Mr. Cleaver, on TV,
I had never seen such a man. It seemed unnatural,
punishing even. Like going to a funeral every day…
although, I was certain these were the men who
made sure all was right in the world and dictated
important letters to pretty secretaries.

Anyway, I showed up for a game or two, was
a late-inning replacement in right field, made an
error, and struck out in my sole turn at bat. Some
boys already knew how to hit and field more than
a little. Figured they were born knowing, which
made me a retard, so I never went back. And that
was that. Then I started watching the Mets like
Cleon Jones and Tommie Agee, and after a while
I picked up on their technique—how they'd watch
the ball all the way to the bat and generate power
and bat speed throughout the hips.

Five thousand plus Major League Baseball games
later, I'd often watch the Yankees with my 11-year-
old niece, Amanda, who proudly wore their team
cap. I'd point stuff out. Other times we'd practice
some. Play catch. Then I'd pitch, she'd hit, and I'd
fetch. So when her softball Raptors were up one and
the dreaded Sea Horses had the tying and winning
runs at the corners with two out in the bottom of the
ninth and a hard grounder was hit to her at third base,
she began the catching-moving-throwing movement
as it approached, moving her feet to get to it and icily
arced a long sidearm throw across the diamond to
first—to beat the runner by a full stride! Coach and
teammates all whooped it up while just outside the
third base line I stomped and waved a fist shouting,
"Yeah, Amanda! Yeah, yeah, yeah! Way to go!"

SALAMANDERS

How he got pinned Woim or why, none of us
knew. He looked regular enough. Like any one
of us slightly older teenaged boys who also lived
in the projects. Fact is, we didn't know or care
what his real name was, or if he even had one.

One day, out of the blue, he approaches us and
boldly says, "I don't go by *that name* anymore."
As if he ever had a choice in the matter. "Okay...
Woim." He must've been about 17 when I heard
that he got drunk and drowned at Orchard Beach.

Following every summer rain thereafter, a putrid
odor of unknown origin would rise and linger in
the projects and the grounds would be littered with
wriggling worms. Figured it somehow had to do
with the death of Woim, but kept that to myself.

Decades later, the cool air soothed as I walked
through a lush park following a summer rain. Trees
and flowers...but most pleasing was that there was
no else around. I felt a sense of wonder. Like when
I was a little boy in the Catskills after a summer rain...

The cool air smelled green. Tingling mist tickled.
On the dirt road by the woods tiny orange dragons
appeared. Soft yellow-underbellies. But when I
stepped out of the park onto the busy city street,
for no apparent reason Woim popped into my head.

He'd been dead a year or so, when I learned the girl
I was out on a date with was his sister. Pretty, with
waist-length black hair, Joanna wore a white sundress.
She seemed obsessed with St. Francis of Assisi. As
far as obsessions went, I figured, a damn good one.

At the movies we saw actors dot vast wheat fields in
Days of Heaven. She smelled of garlic, but I didn't care.
Said she was devoutly Catholic like her Puerto Rican
mom. Her father, a Czech gypsy, had long since aban-
doned them. Joanna Redzosko...Woim...Redzosko.

Simeon

Joseph was our old father's favorite,
whom all ten of his brothers hated.

A too-precious-to-shepherd-with-us
seventeen-year-old dreamer,
who'd stroll about in his multicolored coat
that the great old man had bestowed upon him.

Hubris-filled and foolish, he
boldly announced his dreams—
of our obeisance to him…!

Camped far from our land of Hebron,
we ten fed father's abundant flock of sheep—
when the dreamer appeared.

As natural as the river runs—
we would slaughter the favored son.

Tip his carcass into a deep dark pit.

"No bloodstains!" Reuben exclaimed.

From Joseph's unblemished back—
we tore the multicolored coat.
Screaming murderously, he kicked up a storm.
But as though he were a dung-packed sack—
we slung him—and he plummeted down—

Let him *dream* his death!

A Jewish Giant at Home with his Parents
in the Bronx, N.Y. 1970

On the photograph by Diane Arbus

bare bulb in a wall lamp
tall vertical rectangular wall moldings
plaster streaked ceiling cracks
slip-covered club chairs and couch
plastic covered lampshades
freshly vacuumed old carpet
lackluster curtains (closed)
2 generic paintings and
a console TV

But foremost—upright! An untapped continent. An oxygen-inhaling colossus.
Perfectly proportioned. Complete with horse's neck and tree trunk wrists.

But why brother, why?

Sorely stooped and donning the mocking mask of the eternally defeated?

Of me? You?! Asks the electrified face of the frumpy little yenta, glare fixed
high—on her son.

At her shoulder, the small and formal father spaces: *Pinochle by Hy's at seven
o'clock.* Hands in pockets, he absently faces his son's abdomen. Resigned to this
picture-taking monkey business.

My dear giant:
I'd lay 2 to1 you don't need that cane and orthopedic shoe,
nor slingstone and faith in Yahweh to have slain Goliath.
Shake the dead weight of days from your nuclear shoulders.
Tell *them* you're going out job-hunting.
Fuck one hundred hardcore hookers.
Bust some heads that need busting—

unleash the fury
unleash the fury
unleash the fury,

unleash the love

GOD'S HONEY

Bred to shop, she bled on God.
And was guided by His signs to her.

                exquisite
                gold blizzard
                woolen curls
                liquid sky
                blue eyes she
            stood long arms
                sides holy
                bible tight
                in right hand
                pearl white silk
                button-down
                blouse unbut-
            toned shawl-like
                over nar-
                row shoulders
                draped upper
            back slack sleeves
                fell past slight
                breasts slender
            presence weight-
                less angel
            sequined cream
                body shirt—
                black velvet
                hip huggers—
                naked neck
                natural
            scented swan—

Could tell, by talk she'd talk,
daddy was a millionaire—
Could tell, by her walk in my heart,
she should have been around
when Jesus walked—following him—

A sparrow on each of her bony shoulders—

The Essential Dentistry of Dr. Jack Kreeger

Former Bronx Golden Gloves
bantamweight contender,
toothless and fit, old Dr. Jack Kreeger
is the last affordable dentist.

Mirthful, manic-laugh-loud,
he floats around his spacious office
calling all men "my brother" and all
women "my sister" or "princess."

Refuses to wear a mask, refers all
root canals out, and has the genius to
surround himself with beauty—
an all-peachy Puerto Rican girl
intern and office staff.

Ambitious dental-hygienist,
silky, sing-song-speaking Gloria
drills my upper right bicuspid.

Next week, Dr. Kreeger will extract
my throbbing lower left molar,
without the standard, self-serving
teeth will shift dental bullshit.

"Beautiful! Beautiful!" shouts Dr. Kreeger,
exhaling Beef Lo Mein breath
directly into my wide open mouth
as he reviews Gloria's work up close.

I agree.

Eyeballing the rope-like scar across
my neck and having heard my breathy
rasp, he earnestly asks,
"Teddy, my brother, what happened?"

So I tell him.

He replies, "That they got everything,
is all that matters."

Seizing the pity price moment I pounce,
"Yeah, but I have exorbitant medical bills."

"Listen motherfucker," he chortles,
"you're lucky to be alive!"

The Day Before Christmas

Dumped horizontal, curbside,
between the high-rent high-rise
and my orphan heart,
a long, conical, dark-green-needled pine,
on a frozen bank of auto-exhaust-frosted black snow.

Did they get their dates mixed up?
Upgrade to a bigger one?
Want you to think you've got your dates mixed up?

Or what?

Professor Stephen Niemeyer

This morning they came for the books. Two bearded young men, their hands filled with shopping bags. Five large mahogany bookcases full. Mathematics. And the treasures of my late beloved wife, Maria. Music and literature. Eighty with arthritic hips, I am resigned to be moving to a first-rate assisted-living facility. Except for some seminal volumes I removed and stacked to the side, I told them all books go. Over and done with. Payment received. Not that I *need* the money. Nor am I pressed to vacate. But scheduling weeks in advance in order for the university or a charity to pick up tripped my screw-up detector. No space for a library and of course less privacy. Sentimentality does not serve me. Maria gone and our son and his growing family thriving in Iowa. What an old fool I am keeping our family tradition of a Christmas tree. On this day before Christmas I insisted that the young beards dispose of the tree. They also took the book stack I had placed to the side. Probably felt entitled since I made them take the tree.

ONE DAY IN NOVEMBER

Carafe of black coffee.

Tweak a villanelle. Read *The Complete Idiot's Guide to Reinventing Yourself.*

Turn on clock radio. A possessed man shouts his truth: "ALTHOUGH RESULTS MAY
VARY YOU HAVE NO CHOICE BUT TO LOSE WEIGHT WHEN TAKING FAT
ABSORB NO CHOICE!"—

Take half a nap. Take a piss. Complete the nap.

Gulping OJ, plan my day—a leisurely walk through Central Park to the P.O.

On the street engage—posted atop her stoop—old wheelchair-bound widow Julia about
how she fared playing the slots in AC.

At the park's archway entrance, a rakish dachshund and a yawping cross between a
Pekinese and a fly wrestle each other into an ass-sniffing knot.

Walk in. Walk on…kick back on a bench. Flawlessly clashing Fall colors. Dread black
at five. The brown 9x12 envelope resting on my lap contains my screenplay contest entry
and sacrificial $15.00 reading fee. Oh well…

owe it to myself. Still,

should have sprinkled anthrax on the manuscript. And what's this puny plaque affixed to
backrest of bench? Bestowed by Mr. and Mrs. Leo Bagatelle? What?! The city can't
afford to pay for its own benches? Why couldn't the Bagatelles spray-paint their tag onto
a subway car? And why should I need to see my name crawl across some yummy
starlet's nakedness?

Why not?

Relax shoulders. God's cool air caresses nostrils. Flows in and out and in and out and in
and out…flushing head. Like a shadow, slip out of myself. And watch…

Letter to Lori Waterhouse

for Amy Foster

The tip off: When, outside your ventilator- and sole daughter-dependent, old mother's hospital room, you cast unblinking, glazed, rainbow-green eyes on yours truly and your longtime friend Judith (don't call me Judy) Pizzutti, and said, "I probably shouldn't say this, but you two look good together." And so, I became a burnt offering. But really, Judith Pizzutti?! Joyce Starr…maybe. Yeah, Miss Starr. Star…like the star-saturated, boundless, black sky we marveled at that late August night in Ogunquit as we lay supine in chaise lounges on the back lawn side by side. Falling meteoroids turned into trails of blazing light in our atmosphere. Thirty-three murky years since I had last seen even a single star, until that night we shared. Rebirthed, beneath the four-and-a-half-billion-year-old night light of Cassiopeia, Hank Williams, and you—my aurora Lori. Last night I dreamt I awoke and saw your doll face with my one open (left) eye—and felt warm inside, knowing you were replenishing yourself sleeping safely by my side. But I must confess, I long ago discarded my fleece-lined, ear-flapped, green camouflage L.L. Bean hunting cap we got to match. But hope I've held on to a few of the IQ points I gained from the forehead-to-forehead osmosis. And still have your (no longer state of the art) video camera that you never asked me to return. And the *whys* of my immortal love could roll easily on off my fat tongue, but the prevalent reason for this epistle is to *tell you* something I may otherwise *never* get the chance to. That is, in retrospect, how quietly clear it is that I was the compact and rather suave Gomez to your wonderfully aloof and statuesque Morticia. John Astin and Carolyn Jones, the original TV version of course. And like Gomez, I would have planted kisses from your fingertips to your shoulder on your most accessible arm several times each and every day. So I'm telling you *now*.

The Healing

Last night I killed my father. A garrote. Pulled his neck back with the force of a TV set falling from a 6-story rooftop and his legs flew up and he landed flat on his back. Dead before he hit the floor, he never saw it coming. Did him in the very bedroom of my conception. I don't recall a thud.

TO THE LIGHT, DARKLY

News that Bill Gates is no
longer the world's richest man
shook me.

I was moved to contemplate
man's place in the universe.
God's accordion.

Our tiny mortal minds are
hard-wired for linear time.

Time exists only relative
to constant speed of light.
Einstein's violin.

Mind is a sense.
Like sight, taste, hearing,
smell, and touch.
No more, no less.

Because I think I am?
Am what?

Parting the flooded Jordan River
was God's final meddle into
men's affairs.

Minor personal miracles occur:
Deeds of dangling spirits of dead.

In time we die.

Like my neighbor down the hall,
Mrs. Scirghio, said after her husband
died choking on a chicken bone:

"When ya numbuz up, ya numbuz up."

Eternity is a conceit.

Absence of time
is not eternity.

Every breath is.

Straight Lines

My mother said I should be afraid of my own shadow. My father said I should ram my fist deep down a big wet red dog's throat. A dignified old lady neighbor said I was a nice boy. Go fuck yourself, I replied. Hot shit Petey Cooney said I was real shit because I dropped a pop fly. Miss Pakula said I was smart in school. The palmist took one long look at my palm, said nothing. Stared sadly at me, and split. My grandmother said I was a doppelganger. My grandfather who escaped the Nazis, said I was a Nazi. Mike Gucci at 7 Santini Bros. Moving & Storage Co. said I couldn't do anything right. The white detective with the yellow eyes said the many teeth marks on the dead girl's broken body were mine. My Uncle Saul said I should flee to Israel. My Uncle Jerry said I should go to law school and get married. A state appointed Pakistani psychiatrist said I was a paranoid schizophrenic. Alison Katz said my dick was too small. Alison Katz said my dick was too big. A Korean hooker said I had a nice dick. The most guarded person I've ever met, said I was the most guarded person he's ever met. Lucy Reyes said I was talented, had a full head of hair, and knew how to treat a lady. Helen Bannister said I was the most horrible man she'd ever met. An old friend said I had nothing to die or live for. Said my poetry was old and tired. That I need to bathe regularly and get a girlfriend. *Whatever you say.*

Stories

From the Diary of a Prizefighter

In all twenty-six years of my life the government never did shit for me. And that's OK. But I will not allow them to be business partners of mine. Today, in 1983, I work only for me. Nights, in a four-door 74 Ford Fairmont which I turned into a gypsy cab a few months after coming out of a weeklong coma.

The coma shut-down my promising boxing career. I was an up-and-coming white middleweight with a professional record of 8-0, when less than thirty seconds into my first fight on cable TV, a four-round preliminary match in Vegas, that plodding Panamanian deliberately head-butts me right above my left eye. Blinded bloody instantly, I couldn't see the right-hook into my chin that immediately followed. And the referee sees this head-butt as unintentional.

Anyway, this cab business suits me okay. I'm my own boss. I call no man boss. It's against nature, or my nature. Working nights, less people around. And that's good, because something about most everyone bothers me. Especially, if they bring up that fight. Like the other day, I'm walking on Broadway and a sprightly old-timer approaches me. "Aren't you?" he starts to ask, before I cut him off—

"Look," I say, down into his obviously many times broken old nose, "I don't know you, and you don't know me. Let's keep it that way." The hurt look in his eyes…he probably was an ex-fighter. For the rest of the day, I couldn't shake it.

It's not like I've got anyone else to support—so the money's okay. Six nights, ten till six. I don't knock myself out working long shifts. Knock myself out? HA!

I cruise Upper Manhattan, Harlem, and the South Bronx. This includes Washington Heights, the Dominican neighborhood where I live.

My work starts with a pick up of whores from ghetto rooming-houses and residential hotels on West 145th Street, in Black Harlem. I shuttle them to Hunts Point, an industrial part of the South Bronx just a quick trip across the Harlem River, connected to the south-east Bronx by a short bridge.

Having grown-up down in Manhattan's Meatpacking District, nothing was new to me. So I knew, because of their size and Adam's apples, that many of these full-breasted girls were actually chicks with dicks. Chicks, or chicks with dicks, no matter. No tip. But they are regular business.

Anyhow, as far as the chicks with dicks—considering all the shit they have to go through—I respect their commitment to perversity. Besides—as far as I'm concerned—a blow-job is a blow-job is a blow-job. Anyway you cut it. Cut it?! HA! I'm glad mine wasn't!

During the winter months open bonfires burn in corners of block long vacant lots in the wholesale fruit market that is Hunts Point. Fires surrounded by gatherings of warming whores. The whores wait for cruising johns, who pull up in cars and trucks, to signal them in. How do they fuel their ceaseless all-night bonfires? Coats open to showcase bare hormone tits, they shake their bodies around for more warmth. As though they were possessed by thousands of live tongues of lizards— while their fire burns like bright, flashing, orange razors. Smoke rising into cold gray.

Sometimes, I feel like joining these amazingly tall stiletto-heeled warriors in their supernatural shimmy surrounding their fire. Maybe we could pull one of these doughy faced johns from his car and toss his flabby ass into the fire and dance and scream in exaltation, muffling his cries. And if he survived, he'd have the burn scars for the rest of his fucking life. A constant reminder of how, on a cold winter's night in the South Bronx, a black tribe of chicks with dicks along with a titless white prick fed him to their roaring bonfire. What fucking shame. Like getting knocked into a coma on TV?

A couple nights a week local men gather at Hunts Point job sites, in order to get work unloading crates of fruit from incoming tractor trailers. The pay is five dollars per hour, only about a third of what I net driving, but in order to stay in some kind of shape and share in the camaraderie I often join them. Really, I need to start roadwork again. And then the gym. Or maybe I'll apply to City College and take up writing, journalism maybe. Hell, I bet I've read a lot more than most of these college kids.

After knocking off from an unloading shift at two a.m. one night I noticed a very-slow moving station wagon passing by. On its roof, stacked but not tied down, were wooden pallets. Those used to hold the crates of fruit while in the truck, and then discarded by the truckers after the unloading. From about thirty hazy yards, I now observed the station wagon lazily pulling over at a corner curbside gathering of whores by a dying bonfire. I took two steps closer, and squinting, observed a black man in an ankle-length down coat and a furry ear-flapped hunting cap emerge from the driver's seat into the cold. He shoved the unbound pallets off the roof of his station wagon. Onto the sidewalk, crashed the wooden load. The guy looked to be about the same height as me, five-ten. But even factoring out the bulky coat, I could tell that he was exceptionally broad. In exchange for the pile of pallets he was handed some bills by a towering, open-coated (to showcase big bare tits), dicked chick. As the deliverer of pallets turned to get back into the car the street-light struck his face so that I recognized him as Kent. A hard-bodied wall of a fortyish guy I'd run into at the nearby 24-hour Dominican bodega. He'd often be standing up front, looking out, while killing time sipping from a container of coffee. Now I knew why I'd sometimes see him buy several packs of various brands of cigarettes, assorted junk food, and small bottles of under-the-counter Dominican rum. I don't recall who initiated the salutations originally, but we would exchange "hey mans."

"Hey man," I said while approaching him in the bodega the very next night.

"Hey man," replied Kent. He had one of those naturally gravelly voices black men sometimes have.

Respectfully, I then added, "That's some gig you've got supplying the girls with pallets to fuel their fires."

It was as though he had been waiting to talk for some time because with great gusto he bragged that he charged the girls ten dollars a load of pallets, and since there were several of these rapidly burning bonfires going all-night, business was brisk and very profitable. He also made money from the resale of the items he bought for the girls at the bodega. And his eyes glistened as he stated, "I don't allow no competitors."

He asked me if I would like to join him now for the short ride to the vacant lot where he picks-up the loads of pallets. Said he wanted to talk to me about something. I got the feeling he knew who I was, that's why he had confidence in me, but that he was not one to bring it up if I didn't. But as I stepped into the passenger seat I had no idea what he wanted to talk to me about.

Right after he revved up the old station wagon's engine, I found out. He told me that in about a month he was going down to South Carolina for two weeks and wanted me to "consider filling-in" for him for that period.

"I'll need to think about it," I replied, honestly.

"You keep everything you make," he said slowly, to underscore the absence of kickback. "Two-hundred clear, a night. Nice and easy. Plus free sex."

Sex?! I thought to myself. What the fuck's he talking about? He must mean with one of the few real girls. Or, a long term ex-con, which he likely was, probably fucks them all in the ass. No way, I assured myself, was he implying that I am one of those who enjoys the COMPLETE versatility a chick with a dick has to offer.

"I dig a blow-job from just about any of these whores—which I sometimes accept in lieu of fare—but that's as far as it goes," I said.

"Whatever . . ." he replied, offhandedly.

If he had not replied, the issue would have been closed. "Whatever" did not close it for me. "You know man," I said, "I came up in the Meatpacking District, 16th on the far West Side, lots of wild shit. A few of us teenage boys would get blow-jobs from a tall, lean, neighborhood Cuban chick with a dick, who'd socialize with passing friends and neighbors from out her ground floor window. She was a prostitute, but would do certain teenage boys she dug on for free. Her name was Perfecta. I was sixteen. Never paid.

"So," I continue, speeding up my delivery to get to the point, "it's just me and her, on a hot summer's night, in her apartment. Stopped by hoping for a quick blow-job on the way home after a whole day of stocking the dairy aisle at Daitch Shopwell. Perfecta poured us each a rum and Coke. I think she spiked mine, because I passed out right on her bed...

"I was awakened to a feeling of something hard pressing up against my bare ass. Perfecta had pulled down my pants and rolled me over and was trying to fuck ME in the ass! Turned quickly onto to my back and slugged the naked Perfecta square in the face with my right fist—knocking her off the bed onto the floor, and drawing blood.

"'Motherfucker!' she screamed, rising unsteadily to her feet. 'You take blood from my face, now I keel you!' Pulling up my pants, I'm running out of her apartment, with her—after very quickly grabbing herself a weapon from the kitchen—chasing me out into the street."

At this point, we arrive on the lot. Kent asks me to keep on with my story. Which was good, because I had no intention of stopping—

"We're squared off in the street. Me, bare-chested and pants opened at the waist, and this titted, tall Perfecta with her considerable dick—NAKED—ready to bash my head in with a steel bar. Well, I remember feeling relieved that it wasn't a machete she had—because on the street I don't run.

"A girl who'd been sitting on her front stoop smoking and saw it all go down, would later tell me that everybody hanging outside very quickly crowded around this freaky face-off and was going fucking crazy. I have no memory of that, because I was completely locked in on the armed Perfecta—

"'Motherfucker, I keel you!' shouted the bloody faced Perfecta, swinging the bar at my head. I pulled back to dodge the blow, and when the bar slowed down as it finished its arc, I stepped in and snatched it away with my right hand. Held it like a spear and chased her ten or so yards as she fled back into her apartment. Everyone knew I could have caught up and destroyed her, but chose not to. I did knock out her front window with the end of the bar and chucked it back into her apartment. Then I heard sirens. Ran home."

"Funny shit," said Kent, nodding approval.

"It ain't quite over."

"Say what?" said Kent, surprised.

"Well, the next day I'm told by a buddy of mine that I'd better watch my back, because supposedly Perfecta had taken out a contract on me. For the next few weeks, I had to keep looking over my shoulder. It was a drag. So I bought a bottle of Cuba Libre Rum for her, and through this same buddy arranged for a peace meeting. On my way over to her place I also bought a liter of ice-cold Coke. She blew me."

Wordlessly, we now exited his station wagon.

There were hundreds of dumped pallets in the lot. I helped him load and we headed to a dying bonfire surrounded by the girls. As soon as we pulled up and got out, a regular, red-headed, black chick, flashing bare skinny legs, in hot pink hot-pants and a red bikini top, approached Kent. Pointing at a wisp of a girl who stood shivering by a corner bonfire less than half a block away, she asked, in a shockingly high-pitched little voice, for permission to "cut that high yaller little bitch who dissed me."

"OK," replied Kent, without any inquiry. "But don't cut her so she can't work!"

As Kent sent the load of pallets crashing onto the sidewalk, I observed two six-foot-plus chicks with dicks sharing a laugh. One caught me eyeing them and blew me a kiss. Unlike the regular girls, they need no man to provide them with protection. If provoked, they would, without any hesitation, shred your face with a razor that they kept stashed on their person, easily accessible. Inexplicably, a warm flash of affinity with these chicks with dicks passed through me. I got scared. And I don't get scared.

Kent pocketed his payment, and we got back into his station wagon. I wasted no time. "Kent," I said, "I appreciate your offer to fill-in for you but I can't commit to it".

"Hey man, absolutely YOU do not get involved in any shit between the bitches."

I said it as it hit me, "If a chick can have a dick, then a fighter can change his ID and fight in another state."

"What the fuck you talkin' about man?"

Don't Blame Me

At three-thirty on the sixteenth of September the first of two open to the public (free) Yom Kippur 5763 Yizkor services at Temple Beth Torah would begin. And, stated the recorded phone announcement, to ensure entry it's advised you arrive (to wait in line outside the temple) half an hour before.

From past experience, I knew, that at three-twenty-five (five minutes before starting time) entry tickets would be distributed to the first two-hundred-eight people in line. If you were not among this first group of entrants you'd have to remain in line another hour for the second and final free service (tentatively scheduled for four-thirty) to begin. This arrangement eventually accommodated all of the close to four-hundred worshippers who'd show up on this holiest of all Jewish holidays for the free Yizkor service, which memorialized closely related dearly departed.

Since age fourteen, twenty-nine years ago, I may have missed one year due to an eight-thousand-pound depression. Otherwise, every year, in honor of my beloved mother I'd make it my business to attend a Yizkor service on Yom Kippur.

To make sure I'd gain admission to the three-thirty service, I arrived two-thirty, a full hour early. About fifty people were already in line, on the Second Avenue side of Temple Beth Torah, when I took my place this sunny, very warm afternoon on the Upper East Side of Manhattan. Jacket already off, I loosened my tie and unbuttoned the top button of my shirt, feeling fortunate to be situated under the shade of a small tree. Resigned to stand and wait an hour, alone, I'd let time pass, alternately observing the stream of passersby and the gabby line gatherings to the front and rear of me. The gabby line gatherings proved to be far more interesting.

Directly before me stood a threesome consisting of a short, sturdy old man in a peaked cap, a frumpy, fifty-something woman, and a pushing-thirty version of the frump. The old man impressed me. Although he had a hearing-aid in each ear and that fossilized look of the truly old, he stood erect and looked pain free. He had to be well into his eighties. And that burnt me because it brought to mind that for the past month, summoned down to Bonita Springs Florida, grinding herself into dust attending to the needs of her helpless, hospitalized, stroke-stricken, seventy-year-old mother, was the woman I love.

Behind me, was an instantly forgettable couple. Never would they need to don masks if they paired as bandits.

In a gabby gathering just ahead of the threesome before me, I spotted the sensational cream-colored face of a young blond woman. Dreamy, fragile, and ready. Like a Sixties Marianne Faithful. I could always stare at *her*. That this young woman, attired appropriately for the occasion in a modest brown shirtdress, had the torso of a tree stump did not have to come into play—

"I'm not even going in," shrilled a male voice into the back of my head, "and I'm pissed at this friggin' system." Turned around, it was Mr. Instantly Forgettable into his cell phone.

"That's why you're pissed!" I blurted at him. And turned back around. What a putz. The temple is providing a perfectly good service in an organized manner to non-members, and the system is no good? Like he, Mr. Instantly Forgettable, could come up with a better system. Better for who? Him. And what the fuck's he doing waiting in line if he's not going in. Keeping his female counterpart company, I guess. If you're going to do that just keep your trap shut and do it. And who could be on the other end of a call like that? His mother?

The frump was now addressing the frumpette, "You should have asked them to get up." The frumpette, it seems, had accompanied the old man up to the three reserved—for the elderly and infirm—benches by the entrance, but all seats were taken. "But he," responded the frumpette, head gesturing at the old man, "said not to. That it was okay."

I'll gladly get one of those thoughtless cows to get up, I felt like interjecting. But figured it's not my business to overrule what the old man had told the frumpette. Anyway, the sturdy old man, jacket in hand, now walked away with the frumpette. Leaving the frump to hold their place in line. I told the frump I'd hold their place if she wanted to join them. No thanks, said the frump. Who went on to inform that the frumpette was her daughter. And the old man, her father. He was up visiting from his suburban Philadelphia home. Ninety-six years old, he retired from his career as gym teacher at seventy-three. A widower, he refused to move to a retirement community. Her only concern was his driving. And being that he lived in the suburbs he had to drive some. *Ninety-six.*

"God bless him," I officiously pronounced, and shifted my sights beyond her to Marianne Faithful Face. She was chatting with a taller, bare shouldered, collagen-lipped brunette. They faced a wavy-brown-haired, squat man, his back, for the most part, to me. In a navy blue suit, he stood at ease between the two. Closer to Marianne Faithful Face. Husband, brother, or chiropractor. Very possibly, two of three. When the conversation appeared to shift away from her, the brunette began licking around her enhanced lips. Deflation anxiety? Twice around with tongue, before doing an about face to feature her—thanks to tight black stylish pants—anti-gravity butt. More man-hunter than mourner, for this somber service a burka, in my opinion, would've been more appropriate attire.

Speaking of burkas, the entire curb was blocked off by four-feet-high cement barricades to prevent against the possibility of Jew-hating terrorists crashing an explosives-loaded van into the temple. Four formidable plain-clothes (jacket and tie) clad security guards were privately hired to work the event. Retired cops. Two were stationed in the entrance. And two worked the avenue. Alongside a bus stop, about twenty feet up ahead of me, I noticed the frumpette and the old man sitting atop the ass accommodative flat surface of the cement barricade. Beneath a pitiless sun, leisurely they chatted, as city busses rolled up and away bathing the twosome in the most noxious fumes the city has to offer. With certainty, I'd wager, that one hit of that bus exhaust is worse for your health than 30,000 years of second-hand cigarette smoke. And I loathe cigarette smoke. Ninety-six-years-old and he couldn't care less. *Damn.* I'd have to go back to my teenage years to sit unbothered in what was an open air gas chamber. Not being overly concerned about things had to be the longevity key.

"Look at him sitting there," I excitedly urged the frump, pointing at him after tapping her shoulder, "he's like a teenager!" And hoped, immediately after saying it, that I didn't curse him with the evil eye. The frump smiled. I'd have felt a lot better if she'd have *pooh, pooh, poohed* at him (it had to be three times), like my mother (who was from a small dirt poor shtetl in Poland) would on me, following it with *kenna hora** if someone tossed a flattering comment my way.

Not only does this double talisman not hurt, I daresay it is vital. This is because, very commonly, unconscious human envy is hidden beneath words of good will. Left unchecked in the air these words are live negative energy. This negative energy often can survive just long enough (a matter of seconds) to infiltrate one of the eternally wavering, otherwise impotent, air rampant, deathly spirits that witness us. Symbiotically merged, this force of misfortune slips simply into the soul of the accursed. As simply as the spirit slips from the body when one gives up the ghost. Anyway, I got good and lost. . . after forcibly carrying off Ms. Marianne Faithful Face and her ass offering associate. . . .

Snapped to when one of the plain clothed security guards said—excuse me sir—to me and handed me a ticket for entry. The two women had apparently been in my depraved custody for close to forty minutes!

In back of me, a shrill male voice complained about "this system." It was, of course, Mr. Instantly Forgettable. Complaining to Mr. Ticket

---

* Yiddish - *may the evil eye stay away*

Distributor, who was in the process of handing him an admission ticket. Mr. Ticket Distributor completely ignored the words of Mr. Instantly Forgettable. He was a genius.

Within two minutes the line started to move. The frumpette and her grandfather returned. As though I mattered not, a robust gray couple waving their tickets cut right in front of me. I let it slide because they were senior citizens. And, more importantly, because I needed to adjust into a prayerful mindset—

"I'm a Jewish person! You can't do this!! I'm a Jewish person!" Came the yells from the entrance. The two women doing the yelling were being blocked from entering the temple by a security guard. Apparently, this ticketless twosome had shamelessly rushed the entrance. Middle-aged, layered in make-up, and sporting fresh bouffant hairdos, I could sense these weren't merely East Village-chic invaders out for an afternoon frolic, or simply result-oriented yenta perpetrators, but the real deal—the unconquerably insane. From my long years in the Bronx, I knew the type very well. They are the handful of white people left in certain Bronx neighborhoods (Pelham Parkway for one), not counting the influx of Albanians, Russians, and other assorted East European immigrants who appeared during the nineties. All day, they hang-out in Burger King loudly swapping stories of their imagined rendezvous with movie stars, while easily digesting Whoppers chased with coffee. Nighttime often brings about a shift in venue to a rowdy bingo parlor for an evening of gaming or an otherwise empty dump of a diner for extended hours of very minimal ordering and plenty of harmless delusional conversation. What drew this duo—never before seen in the area—to Temple Beth Torah this Yom Kippur? Who knows? Maybe they were looking for me. They do enjoy a good outing. Anyway, a gentleman on scene at the face-off, who must've been and an elected officer of the temple, intervened, advising the security guards to allow the two ticketless line-busting sisters of screwiness to enter. Terrorists, they weren't. Like the security guard who completely ignored Mr. Instantly Forgettable, he was a genius.

The line then moved smoothly. And as was the case with all in line who preceded me, when I reached the front I had to stop momentarily in order for a security guard to perfunctorily wave a metal-detecting wand down away from my body before being permitted to enter the temple.

The vast makeshift room of worship was filled with rows and rows of pre-arranged folding chairs. One of the first fifty or so entrants, I pounced upon an empty aisle seat closest to the exit. In another part of the temple was the main room, which was where services for members (payers of a considerable annual fee) were held. That room had cushioned benches and stained glass windows. Which is not to say that there was anything wrong with the well air-conditioned makeshift room. Up front, we had a podium. Several feet to its left and slightly to its rear was an ark containing two torahs. The room filled fast. Not much jockeying around. Within a couple minutes, few seats remained available. Looking around, I realized that the two sisters of screwiness were not yet in the room. They must have gone straight to the ladies room for extensive powdering. *Fuck*, one of the few empty seats is to my immediate right, practically in my lap. One of them will probably come in and sit there! Her crazy vibes destroying my prayerful mood. And in they marched— past me—to the other side of the room. Where they had to sit apart, but could at least be in the same section. If either would've taken the seat next to me I'd surely have retreated to the back of the room and stood for the entire service. With warm welcoming eyes, I greeted the old woman who came in and sat down next to me.

A reform synagogue, the men did don yarmulkes but the cantor was a young woman (and not bad-looking). She sang the King James version of Psalm 23 sweetly, *The Lord is my shepherd…*As soon as she finished, the carefully coiffed, pleasantly plump, youthful-looking rabbi calmly adjusted his tallis, before launching into a pat and flat spiel about some former classmate of his named Davidoff…Cancer…Not pausing, as chairs shuffled and chatter broke out on the other side of the room. I had not expected the two sisters of screwiness to act up during the service, and when I looked over to the other side of the room I spotted each of them seated apart quietly. From my vantage point, there was no discernible pocket of ruckus. The disturbance ceased as quickly as it started. Not missing a monotonous beat, on spoke the rabbi…Stopping not, a few minutes later, when, in through the door burst a couple of beefy EMS men going directly past him to the renewed shuffling and buzzing coming from the other side of the room.

Toward the rear, in the far aisle of that side of the immense room, I recognized the frump and frumpette standing among six or seven loosely huddled people. Collectively, the group took on the form of a protoplasm. In the middle of a row close to the protoplasm, the two EMS men eclipsed the seated person to whom they were attending. A minute later (the rabbi was plodding on about Davidoff's brave battle), the protoplasm split, allowing the EMS men to walk the dwarfed and bewildered, white tee-shirted, ninety-six-year-old, frump/frumpette progenitor through. At both sides the old gentleman was supported by an EMS man gripping him beneath each armpit as they continued on, slowly stepping several steady paces up the aisle, before he collapsed slack into their strength. Totally self-absorbed, the rabbi took a breath (having buried Davidoff, he somehow was not yet finished) when, coincidentally, directly past him en route out, the old man was carried. One EMS worker gripped him under his armpits and the other by his ankles. The body sagged like a hammock beneath the weight of a slumbering suburbanite. Sheepishly, the frump—*she'd volunteered his age, I'd NEVER have asked*—and frumpette followed. The rabbi reacted to the glum procession before him with a momentary look of blank indifference, before droning on with his speech. A minute or two later, he wrapped up. And I—*I swear*—when I told the frump her aged father displayed the physical ease of a teenager, I wished *not* to curse him.

Ballad of Caleb Belleu

He was ready to give her a goodnight kiss and be on his way, when she invited him in. Right after their first date, a movie, "American Graffiti," up on Fordham Road at the Capri. The Bronx, in April of seventy-three.

He, was Caleb Belleu. An intensely guarded, directionless 18-year-old. And, his nubile brunette date was 17-year-old Shelly Gold. Her house was exactly eight blocks and a park from "the schoolyard" of P.S. 89. Where he hung out, among a dangling bunch of drug wrangling girl conquerors.

Shelly loved the movie and loved him. Why not, Caleb was a naturally-muscled pretty boy who exuded an attractive aura of melancholia. He also was deceptively bright and very respectful. His godmother said he looked like the actor Montgomery Clift.

What he didn't have was a J-O-B. A high school graduate, at times, he talked of college. But talk was all it was.

He'd forgotten the movie as soon as it ended. It was unreal to him. But on the bus ride back to their neighborhood, he told Shelly, he "also, liked the movie a lot."

He did like her. Besides being good-looking and crazy about him, she was smart and smiled freely. A senior in high school, she got good grades. Shelly did not hang out. She was unknown to the guys he hung with.

He had seen her on Allerton Avenue a couple of times, alone, shopping. This afternoon, when he spotted her across the street, he forced himself to approach her. And as his heart tried to pound out of his head, he struck up a conversation. The interest was unmistakably mutual and their "eight—tonight" date set.

That she was unknown to the guys he hung with was of paramount importance to Caleb. He would not have to be a master of eroticism. There was no risk of exposure.

You see, Caleb was a virgin. He was very ashamed of it. He had more than his share of opportunities to change that, but was afraid that word of his virginity would get out. Or, worse yet, he'd fuck up—fucking.

Caleb was born, a bastard, to a loving mother who doted heavily on her sparkling boy. When the child asked about his father she'd say, "I'll let you know the whole story, when you are old enough to understand." An otherwise healthy young woman, she suffered from asthma.

The boy loved his mother very much, but by the time he reached puberty he wished she'd JUST leave him alone. He began breaking away.

The night Caleb was out at his first ever petting party his mother DIED during an asthma attack. He never cried. At the party, shy 13-year-old Caleb had been an intimidated observer. At 18, the shy young man remained—an intimidated observer.

His mother had begged him to stay home that night. But then, she always wanted only him. If only he listened and stayed home that night she . . .

His widowed godmother took him right in, to her two-room housing-projects apartment. Infirm and elderly, she was glad to have him around. They lived off her social security check.

The young man still lived there with her. The cramped apartment was similar to the one he had lived in with his mother, in the adjacent building.

Shelly led Caleb up the carpeted staircase of her sleeping family's upholstered home. Self-conscious, to the point of paranoia, Caleb assured himself that the transformation he was feeling, inwardly, into a grotesque space alien trespasser could not be real and continued to follow Shelly's weakest asset on its ascension to the second floor.

Shelly's room was a soft pink. Shelly was red hot for the blue boy—Caleb. As the blue boy stood, ruminating on how wondrously shiny the doorknob of her closet door was—she jumped him.

Healthy and inexperienced, she had decided it would be Caleb, and it would be now. Apparently, she wasn't concerned about her parents. He surely couldn't be. After all, he was a FUCKIN' MAN, wasn't he?

He had to piss and he pushed her off and excused himself. She told him to tiptoe through the hall to the next door on the left for the toilet. He did. He was extremely uptight. He couldn't piss. He threatened himself with death by violence.

It didn't help.

When he got back to the pink room the hot girl AGAIN jumped him. They groped, kissed, and grinded. The pressure from his bladder was becoming painful. His manhood—flaccid. Caleb excused himself again.

And again, couldn't piss.

He tiptoed back to Shelly's room, cursed with uneasiness concerning her sleeping parents, unowned performance anxiety, and painful pressure from his bladder. She now wanted to put "it" into her mouth. He dropped his jeans to his knees. Had to. She dropped to her knees and put it into her mouth. It had no reaction to her oral action.

"Shel-lee," the phlegmy call of her mother coincided with the flick of the light switch from the toilet. Instantly, Caleb pulled—up—his jeans and Shelly—down—her blouse—rumpled—they sat—apart—on her bed.

"Shel-lee are you o-kay?"

"Yes, mom."

"Did you have a good time?"

Smiling into Caleb's grimace Shelly quickly took his hand and kissed it. She then replied to her mother, "Yes mom."

"Shelly, next time your father and I want to meet Cu-pid."

"Okay, and it's Ca-leb mom, Ca-leb, not Cupid."

"So long as he's white. Goodnight baby."

"Goodnight mom."

When he felt sure that her mother was back in bed he excused himself for the final time, before tiptoeing downstairs and slipping out the front door and Shelly's life, forever.

Ballooned bladder ready to burst Caleb scurried around the corner, stopped, by a blue VW Beetle, unzipped and took his dick out.

Thirty seconds would pass, a second at a time, before he could piss—fire—onto the driver-side door of the Bug.

The piss lasted four full minutes.

Piss rivulets streamed smokily fierce on the black tarred street. The Bug was drowned.

Bladder relieved but sore, Caleb lit a True Blue and took a long sucking drag on its air-filter. Exhaled, and was overcome by an avalanche of emotional inadequacy.

He couldn't piss, he didn't fuck. He was a piece of fuckin' shit.

He needed to get high. Drained of life he bleached white from rageful shame. He began the long thirteen block walk to Bill and Ray's Bar on White Plains Road, where he hoped there'd be drugs to cop.

Midway through his journey Caleb's mood blackened to a depth lower than any he had ever known. One from which, he feared, there would be no return. He walked faster.

It didn't help.

At ten past midnight Caleb arrived at the bar. His dope connection was not there. Caleb badly wanted to snort some dope, but had to settle for three bootleg Tuinals.

Immediately, he split for the bodega on the corner, bought a can of Coke and washed the boots down.

He couldn't face anyone and started aimlessly walking westward, waiting for the boots to kick-in. Three should loosen his speech slurred but leave him fairly functional mechanically. The boots did not disappoint.

Ten minutes later the pilly meltdown of Caleb's hurtin' brain began. The recklessness of the goof-ball head met his already dark agitation. This coupling made Caleb feel like "doing something."

The XXX Globe movie theater was right across the street. He crossed over. Last week a few of the guys dropped acid and went to the Globe to see "The Devil In Miss Jones."

Caleb didn't go. He would never drop acid. He felt certain he'd have a bad trip. As for the movie, to Caleb, watching XXX movies was like watching surgery.

He kept both, his aversion to XXX movies and acid abstinence to himself. He never risked ridicule.

By the Globe, he closely inspected a poster depicting a spread-eagle "Miss Jones," when he felt a hand tapping him gently on the left shoulder.

It was a kid around Caleb's age and height. But blond, chinless, and slight. A complete unknown, "Hi, I'm Peter."

Caleb knew he was being hit on, "Tsup?" he curtly questioned.

Peter stepped back and took a chance, "Do you want to go for a walk?"

"Let's go to the park." Tight and wired Caleb surprised even himself with that reply.

As they walked, less than a block to the park, Peter said, "You're the best looking guy I've ever been with."

Caleb smoked and said nothing.

The park was empty. But, that could change without hardly any notice. Peter dropped to his knees before Caleb, and Caleb dropped his jeans to his knees. Caleb gave up thinking. The night was still and warm. More like summer than spring.

Peter blew better than the whores Caleb had previously gotten blown by. His tongue was loving. Caleb felt manly and defiant. He WAS a man. So much a man, another man was blowing him.

Caleb spurted lightning into Peter's mouth. Satisfied. Caleb WAS a man.

He looked down and suddenly stepped back, sickened. Peter was jerking off. The kid had a real big dick and was releasing mightily. Disgusted, Caleb half-heartedly kicked Peter once in the chest, knocking him on his back. Pulled up his jeans and split.

Caleb knew he wasn't gay and it felt good not to give a fuck. But he did give a fuck.

Temporarily diverted by the experience in the park, his soul torment again howled bloody. Caleb began to hyperventilate. But, quickly managed to get it under control. His head needed a boost.

He got it, back at the bar, in three quick shots of Jack Daniel's. And still had close to fifty dollars on him from a three day job, helping his neighbor, Junior, distribute circulars for a new car wash up in Yonkers. He did not want to run into anyone. Left the bartender a buck tip and split across the street.

There, he hung in front of the busy newsstand and smoked. It was 1:10, but it was Saturday night. Caleb watched as cars pulled-up and were left double-parked in a line, engines still humming as drivers jumped out to pick up Sunday's papers. Obliviousness was settling on him and he gave in to it.

His oblivion was a spacey sort of reminiscence that took him— into the bus coming back from the movie sitting next to Shelly.

Before him was the sun-reddened bald crown of the gentleman's head who was seated directly in front of him.

The ears of the head would—HE—grab and like a beast gone berserk bite down on the baldness and bite and bite . . .

The thought amused him then, and broke him up now. Laughing, he took a few steps toward a—left running—brown Ford Pinto. Stopped laughing, jumped in and drove off!

The car was needed to pick up a hooker from the West Farms streets. Had to FUCK tonight! He had balked, in the past, when it came to fucking a hooker, because he figured that was like putting it into a sewer. He would NOT think that. He also resolved to be cautious with the car, but NOT to think about getting caught.

A guy he knew who could sometimes borrow an uncle's car had recently given Caleb a nighttime tour of West Farms. Like locusts, the hookers had swarmed, blanketing some blocks entirely.

Caleb took a circuitous route, using side streets to get to West Farms. He didn't even turn on the radio. He would fuck and take the subway back. He did turn on the AC. He loved AC. This was going to go right. He didn't give a fuck. It WAS right. The night would become a fond FUCKING memory.

Caleb detoured past the high-profile main strip on Tremont, where he knew hundreds of tough, hardened hookers occupied the prime street real estate.

He cruised a side street in search of an attractive part-time amateur. Once around. That was the plan. No block, would he cruise, more than once.

Immediately, he came upon a small gathering of girls hanging for business. One girl stepped toward him in his stopped Pinto. He waved her off and signaled for one from the rear. Bingo.

124

Long limbed for a small girl—Venus—was slim yet very shapely. She had dark brown skin, full red lips, and a short afro haircut. Caleb found her very attractive.

He would be her first trick of the night. Perfect, he thought, she's fresh. Not yet fouled.

Twenty bucks to fuck and ten more for the hour at the Royal Ostrich Motel.

Done.

Caleb put the Pinto into drive and headed, the couple blocks, to Southern Boulevard. The Royal Ostrich was a few miles north, on Southern Boulevard and 183rd.

For Caleb, Venus had made an exception. She preferred to work, cars only, at ten bucks a blow-job. But, she was taken with Caleb's movie star good looks. And even though she pinned him for being stoned, she could sense that he was no problem.

She could. She could sense if a john was trouble. If she got bad vibes she was OUT of the car.

Unfortunately for Venus, she did not incorporate this intuitive gift into her "private" life. All, her past and present boyfriends were trouble.

She asked Caleb for a cigarette. He dug her saucy little voice and noticed that the green miniskirt and platform shoes she wore did not age her fresh schoolgirl face. He handed her a cigarette. She had a lighter. Venus lit up and smoked.

Feeling good, Caleb asked her, "Do you go to school?"

Venus replied that she had gone to all girls Walton High for two years, before dropping out, "because the school was bugged-out, wild, all bull-dyke bitches." Caleb had heard that about Walton.

She then proudly proclaimed, "I passed the Bronx High School of Science exam."

"So, why didn't you go?"

"I wouldn't have known anyone there, so I asked my father what he thought."

"What he say?"

"He said, 'You have a nice little shape—you'll do fine.'"

Caleb had no response to that, and cruised on through a row of green lights on Southern Boulevard. Venus commented on how good the AC felt.

A rush of love flushsuddened Caleb. He considered running away with her.

Fuck everybody.

At a red light, a McDonald's was on their right. Caleb asked Venus if she wanted to stop for something to eat.

"Maybe," she purred, "after."

In less than two minutes they'd reach the Royal Ostrich, and her reply pleased Caleb.

The light turned green, and as his right foot shifted and pressed gently down on the gas, he laughed to himself, wondering how anyone could come up with a name for a motel as ridiculous as—

"Oh fu-uck!" shrieked Venus, blasting his thought process. A shrill siren mixed hellish with her shriek.

Up in the rear-view mirror Caleb saw a police car flashing him over. Caleb, numbly, pulled over. Bolting from the car, Venus took to flight—

The lone cop leapt out of his car, revolver cocked and drawn— pointed down—by his right thigh.

"Hold it right there!" he shouted at the fleeing girl's back. She kept running. The revolver remained—pointed down—by his right thigh.

Out of his body, mind, and car—it was Caleb—rushing the cop, "She had nothing to—"

The first bullet blew through his arm—another—into his heart. Downed Caleb. Out a tenement window a female voice flew, "Cop shot da keed—dead!" Traffic stopped. Salsa and sirens.

The puddles were red.

Uptown Express

The connecting door in the back of the car clack-bangs open. And an expressionless Asian man, covered like a Christmas tree, with assorted junk, such as glow-in-the-dark yo-yos and ringing kiddy cell-phones emerges. To trumpet his presence, he shakes a brain-banging rattle. And advances cautiously through strap-hanging passengers. Amid whom, I stand.

As he passes I'm tempted to stop him, to tell him how that blood-curdling rattle is exactly what I've been searching for, for the greater part of my adult life. But I restrain myself, realizing he's just another man, like myself, doing what he needs to survive.

A walkman wired kid maintains his pigeon head bop while gesturing to the man for batteries.

Eighty-Sixth and Lex., Manhattan's Upper East Side, is next. It's the stop before Harlem on this Bronx bound number 5 subway. Uptown Express.

It is at this Eighty-Sixth Street stop that I can always assure myself of my psychic powers. I merely will the command, and every white person in the car pours out. Tonight is no different.

At times, I've been tempted to shout that command, "All white fuckers off!" But I'm adjusted too well, or I'm too tightly adjusted. Depends on how you look at it.

The last white man—I am—and maneuver to a mid-car seat vacated by a trim yuppie girl with horsy good looks and a smart black leather briefcase.

It's 8:00 p.m., and only a few people need to stand.

After scanning all for psychotic vibes and untreatable tuberculosis, I deem it safe to shut my tired eyes for the few minutes between stops. Unless, I hear the quick crescendo clack of a connecting door sliding open.

I need to see who gets on at each stop and who enters from between cars.

Surprises, no.

Eyes shut I space, for what could very well be a personal best ten minutes straight, before the train screeches a metallic bone chill into the Harlem station. Where, we come to a jerking halt. More people exit than enter.

Subsequent stops are up the Bronx and local. Frequent and numerous. Eyes open.

A restless teenage boy passes quickly through the length of the car into another and then probably into another.

The empty orange can of Sunkist orange soda rolling on the floor stops by me.

I shove it aside with my foot and looking downward am reminded of the bruised condition of the knuckles on my right hand. On my lap rest my hands.

How the fuck do you bloody your knuckles punching a wall— when you're asleep?

Three stops—in ten minutes—later, we emerge from the bleak tunnel into the night light, high on the el, pulling into Jackson Avenue.

I kick the bruised knuckles out of my head.

At Jackson, the doors to the platform and the connecting door on my far left bang open in unison.

I take a couple seconds to see who's coming and going before looking left, to the back end of the car, where stands a five-feet-tall troll with chest-length, bushy, charcoal-colored hair.

The troll, a female, holds a long red umbrella. Mutters incoherent Spanish and attempts—without warning—to thrust the point of the long umbrella through the forehead of a seated lady, over whom, she stands. Umbrella bayonet.

The seated black lady raises a forearm and blocks the shockingly out-of-the-blue but sluggish attack. Ashen, she sits frozen.

Gripping the umbrella with both hands, like a bayonet, the huntress faces the rest of the car, lengthwise. Outside of yours truly there are only a few others in the car. An old lady seated opposite me, and a couple down the other end absorbed in conversation. The old lady stares at me. I stare at the troll.

As the seemingly wind-blown dark cloud that is troll approaches I swallow the air psychotic.

I remove my wallet from my back right pocket. Over me, the troll now stands. Umbrella alert, I fix a menacing—don't MAKE ME do my duty—glare on the troll and flash my blue Chase Master Card at her—

Terrified, the troll flees into the car up ahead, pausing momentarily, to poke the orange soda can with the tip of her long red umbrella bayonet.

Sighing deep relief, the old lady seated across from me launches into non-stop Spanish at her new best friend—me. She needs to, to expel her troll induced remnant terror. I understand, but I do not understand much Spanish.

Three stops later, at Simpson, she's still at it. And I continue to automatically nod respectful acknowledgment. Although, I'm no longer really listening. When I was listening, I was able to pick up on her strong feelings about two things. One, her desire to retire to Puerto Rico. And two, her dislike of Dominicans.

In the shelter of her forceful chatter, I space. . . .

At East Tremont the old lady rises to exit. In five or so more minutes I'll be getting off. She exits after we exchange good wishes. On rolls the train.

I spot the woman who was attacked by the troll now sitting in the front-end corner of the car. I did not see her move. If the troll returns it will be through that connecting front-door.

I stand, zip my jacket, and walk to the front. There, strap-hanging left-handed, I lean back on the door from which I'll exit. Kill minutes here.

Glance down at my bruised knuckles and it becomes clear. Dream life reflects the human experience. The human experience must be the reflection of yet another dream. The wall had it coming.

Take the few steps over to the woman whom the troll attacked. Tell her I'm real glad she didn't get hurt.

"Bitch comes back I'll light her hair on fire!"

I nod approvingly. That explains the yellow Bic lighter wrapped in her right fist.

The conductor calls, "Morris Park!" Me.

Skip over the gap onto the platform soon as the doors slide open. Into the night. Under a blank sky.

Things Equal to Things Equal Things

After flushing the toilet and washing his hands, O., feeling buoyant and hungry, stepped through the closet-sized foyer, back into the dinette. Before, he had been constipated and hungry.

On the small circular oak dining table was his Chinese take-out meal of beef with orange flavor. A spicy combination of sliced tender beef sautéed in hot pepper sauce with mandarin orange peel flavor, his favorite. Well-salaried (he was an actuary), the reserved, trim and fit, graying bachelor, easily afforded his three room mid-town Manhattan rental and all his meals out. He never cooked. He'd already carefully transferred the food from the cardboard containers into two ceramic dishes—so that it would taste better.

Cold air blew into the room. O. ALWAYS opened the window when he arrived home. He'd replace the old screen that fell out, down five stories into the back alley, tomorrow. He needed air—even in the winter. A motionless pigeon, its back to O., had parked on the window-sill.

"OOGA—BOOGA—FUCKYA—AAAAGH!" war-cried O.—flailing his arms as he mocked a rush at the black pigeon. The pigeon was not instantly alarmed, but, after a moment, flew off. Tickled by his ability to erupt into tongues, the savage tribal warrior sat down to feast.

Funny, he thought to himself, I've been here three years and there has never been a pigeon by my window. Just sparrows. O. forked up a bite-size piece of translucent orange goo soaked beef, and noticed a small dent in the bed of white rice. Two chews, and swallowed the beef. DELICIOUS!

He turned his head left to face the window for a fresh hit of direct cold air and was reminded of the filthy rat with wings, before turning back to his meal and the dent in the white bed of rice. The room darkened before his very eyes. The possibility was screenless. The feathered rat had flown in and peck-dented the rice! It COULD'VE happened. He had failed to protect himself! It happened. He'd come to expect the worst. The rice was bad! But, he had caught it in time. He'd eat the beef. He'd toss the rice—and forget it!

Robbed at gunpoint last year, O. did not at all panic. But, germ torpedoes snowballed invisible. The pigeon had SAT in the rice! How else could you explain such a dent? It was the sweet savory beef that had been pecked—He was ALREADY poisoned!

As YOU would—if a fire were to ignite beneath your seated bottom—O. reflexively sprang from his chair—and shut the sliding window down. Desperate as a cornered rabbit fighting for its very survival, he grabbed both plates (one in each hand), heavy-footed two steps to the small olive-colored plastic garbage receptacle, dumped the food and put the dishes into the sink.

In the bathroom, he now scrubbed his hands before splashing cool water on his sweaty face. Relieved, he was nonetheless plunged up to his neck in self-hate muck. He approached the kitchen sink tentatively.

With a sopping sudsy sponge he washed the dishes in warm water, and was wiping a dinner plate dry with a dish towel—when he was overcome by the realization of his own stupidity. Hot water! He'd HAVE TO repeat the procedure. But this time, he'd think it through in advance.

The pigeon contaminated the food. The food contaminated the plates. The pigeon contaminated the plates. Simple logic. If A=B and B=C then A=C. Things equal to things equal things. An axiom. The pigeon contaminated the food contaminated the plates contaminated the sponge contaminated the dish towel—

The dish towel—here, the hot water application theory hit a snag. The plates and sponge were readily redeemable. If he hand washed the dish towel it would have to be hung to dry. It went into the hamper. After quickly washing his hands with soap and water, he stepped from the bathroom to grab a dish towel from the top shelf of the foyer closet. And then, re-entered the kitchen. Taking no chances, he did not hang the fresh dish towel on the hook over the sink, whereupon the contaminated towel had hung.

His hands were dry and itchy from overexposure to water. So, from a bottom cabinet, he withdrew a pair of yellow rubber gloves. Gloved, O. washed the two dishes and lone fork in hot water with the sopping sudsy sponge. His hands felt clammy and suffocated in the rubber gloves. THE SAME GLOVES HE'D USED TO WASH THE BATHROOM FLOOR THREE WEEKS AGO?! If he were a pinball machine T-I-L-T would've emblazoned his forehead as he blew from his apartment into the hallway carrying the two dishes, fork and sponge, and tossed them down the compactor chute.

Momentarily relieved, in his apartment, he made a mental note that tomorrow he'd HAVE TO replace the sponge and plates, at lunch break or after work. It was too late now, stores were closed. And the rubber gloves, wet, on the floor of the kitchen WET kitchen FLOOR!— ARM INTO CLOSET FOR PARKA—O. fled torturous iron mind spiral reality—

In the street, on he walked, downtown...Stopping, in the East Village, to wolf down a slice of pizza. He then headed back.

Early tomorrow, O. would awaken, face buried in his own warm scent in his pillow. Relieved, that he had not been poisoned by the one bite of savory orange beef. That he had again eluded imminent catastrophe. He'd leave for work, clean shaven and showered. His short shopping list folded neatly into an inner-compartment of his attaché case. Fantasizing, that on this day of comforting drudgery, something, something good, for him, was in the air.

Kiss of Death

Moneyed, young, and full of himself, Manhattan stockbroker Jack Barish strode home up mid-town Madison Avenue, mightily. And why not? His commission pace was well ahead of last year's personal high, he was still only thirty-one, and he was not a bad looking guy. His time had come. Reagan had the White House and Jack had the mid-western blond babes. And come, he did. A long way from his working-class Bronx roots.

As was his habit, Jack ran his right hand back through his thinning hair. Still there. This, he did, without missing a stride. He chuckled, realizing, that on a cold winter's night like this, if his mother had her way he'd still be donning a woolen stocking cap. Pulled down to keep his ears—

"Ya wanna go out?" screeched a female birdy voice, from the vestibule of a Chase Manhattan Bank a few feet from Jack, interrupting his meditative self-adulation in motion. Looking around, he was the only one. She was, indeed, addressing him.

Hookers do not hang around here, Jack thought, as he took in the Afghan coated, shadowy little figure. No way, was she a cop. "How much for up the ass?" shot mind swaggering Jack, fucking around.

"How would you like to get fucked in the ass?" she shot back.

She's got a point, thought Jack. Desperate and crazy enough to solicit him, a stranger, albeit, one clad in a Brooks Brothers cashmere overcoat, at a spot where hooking was not to be done and her asshole is non-negotiable. The maker of deals got a kick out of that.

"I'm going for something to eat," he announced. "Actually, I was going to detour over to the Oyster Bar where they know Jack Barish. But, If you'd like to have something, we can do Chinese or pizza. I'm buying."

"Okay," she replied.

From the dim vestibule, she emerged. Jack was surprised. Whatever kind of addict she was, she didn't look too bad. One or two pimples on a cute but gaunt face. About his age. Big brown eyes beneath big brown curls.

Scanning the surrounding area, up ahead on the other side of Madison by 40th Street, Jack saw a very small Chinese take-out restaurant. Highly unlikely, he decided, that anyone who mattered would walk in on them at that hole in the wall. There, they went to eat. Side by side, they stood by the counter as Jack peeled a lone ten from a roll of twenties, paying for their orders upfront. He received only loose change in return. Taking off their coats and hanging them on back of their chairs, they sat at the orange Formica table for two. Face to face. Not surprisingly, she was very thin. The three remaining tables were unoccupied. His briefcase, he positioned on the floor between his Italian loafered feet.

"How are you?" she emptily asked.

"I'm always good." replied Jack, delivering his stock go-getter.

Beneath the bright fluorescent light, however, what remained of his magnanimous dinner invitation moment, dissipated before a subtle dread yellow hue which surrounded her eyes like a somewhat irregular mask of Zorro. He simply did not want to look at her. Her mere presence rankled him. He considered asking her to sit at another table, but decided that was too cruel. He'd endure. Looking through her, he instead, launched into an anger fueled *you too can do it!* autobiographical monologue—

"I," loudly announced Jack Barish, before repeating in a low, pressed tone, "I...was the only Jewish kid on a tough block. Top it off, I sucked in school. Zero confidence. *Can you believe it...?* Thank God, though, nature took its proper course and I wound up where I belonged—on top. Had my kosher-deli counterman father ever taught me anything about anything manly, or, for that matter, anything about anything, that's the way it always would've been. But you know what? The simpleton did the best he could. No one ever said life is fair!"

"Listen," continued Jack, resting his palms flat on the table as he straightened-up fully in his chair, "the thing is, fate was very kind to me. Like the man upstairs took a personal interest in Jack Barish. And to put what I'm about to pass on to you into proper perspective, I gave you some background. No one really knows that about Jack Barish. Or, that I didn't have *anything* together until after I turned eighteen."

"So there I am, clueless and lonely, the very night before I hit eighteen, thirteen years ago, March 31,1976—to be exact. Amazing... later that night, the *two tools* needed for achieving the American Dream would be revealed to me—*All I ever really needed to know!* At the RKO Fordham, in one, chance, viewing of what turned out to be a totally awesome new movie called 'Rocky'! *Eye of the tiger!* and *Go for it!* And, I absorbed them. *Eye of the tiger!* and *Go for it! Eye of the tiger!* and *Go for it! Eye of the tiger!* and *Go for it!* Father fucked your mouth when you were in the crib? It don't mean shit! Reach for a tool! Reach for a tool! I don't know why I'm even trying to help you."

Two trays of food were then set before them by the hustling counterman.

Unaffected by Jack's lecture, before either of them raised a plastic fork, she asked, "Would you please buy me a Brandy Alexander?"

The timing and outlandishness of this request caused Jack to echo, incredulously, "A Brandy Alexander?" noticing, for the first time, that her big brown eyes moved in concert with each other but seemed to float around unconnected to any other aspect of her being. And it shook his yuppie ass, more than he thought it should—

"Yeah," she snapped, "a Brandy Alexander. I could hop out to the Blarney Stone we passed—off 39th—and bring it back."

Instinctively, Jack firmly replied, "No."

"Why," she taunted childlike, "you afraid I'm gonna cut out with the cash? I'll leave my nice, warm coat here."

It might be warm, thought Jack, but its nice days were gone. "No," he repeated. He knew, she'd observed his cash wad when he paid. That he was left only with twenties. Get a twenty off him, she probably figured, grab her coat, and when he tries to stop her, start screaming how on this cold winter's night this bastard's taking her coat. A situation, from which, he'd walk away.

Shaking her head, sympathetically, side to side, she now advised, "You have to learn to trust!"

He was still laughing when, back, back behind the eyes, jolted back, was he, to the Bronx—

The alley, back of the strip of six-story apartment buildings on Cruger Avenue, the block he grew up on located less than a short block from the number 2 train Pelham Parkway stop on the el, was narrow but long as a football field. Blocked in on all sides by six-story buildings, it was a long slab of sunless concrete. A long, tall fence backed-up by barking dogs fortified the buildings on the other side of the alley. "The Beast," or "Dirty Deuce," as the graffiti covered number 2 train was known, screeched thunderously by every five or so minutes. Its sheer force rocking the skeletal systems of all creatures of vertebrae within that one short block radius. Which included THE ALLEY—

Where son of a cop Clay Phelan hanged cats from fire escapes.

Where soft-spoken Spanish Bill, old and slightly stooped but tall still, in his weathered black ten-gallon cowboy hat, would fix bikes for boys free of charge in hopes of rounding-up a boy from whom he could gain sexual favors.

Where the basement dwelling inbred Woolfolk clan would picnic, between dripping first floor clotheslines beneath a downpour of chimney soot.

Where the ghostly white haired cat-lady would lay food for strays, mumbling about being fired from her job as a Radio City Music Hall Rockette because she refused to spread her legs for Frank Sinatra.

Where Jack joined the chorus of hyenas howling, "PINK BELLY!! PINK BELLY…!!" As they ripped the shirt from a crying boy's back, held him down and took turns SMACK! SMACK! SMACK!! Palm prints, blood streaked, raw, red belly. Laughing Jack, thankful it wasn't him on the receiving end.

Where a guy could take a piss.

Where that angel dust loving, rotten toothed, mudslide, Gerald Fiorino casually approached Jack as he practiced flipping baseball cards and called him a Jew bastard before cold-cocking him with a hip driven left hook to the ear. Five days, counted Jack, till the ear stopped ringing. Kept it to himself. Blessed revenge, he never got.

And where that same motherfucker Gerald Fiorino, arm slung around the slim shoulders of Natalie Ragovey, descended, with her, into. But, not before spotting Jack and Szyk hanging out about ten parked cars down the same side of the block. So he stopped along the way to jerk her tightly to him, whisper in her ear, and showcase a long kiss. Head fixed straight, Jack pretended not to see them. Observing the couple only from the corner of his thirteen year old eye. He would not give hated and feared Fiorino the in-your-face satisfaction.

Jack considered Natalie, who was a year ahead of him in eighth grade and lived directly across the street from him, to be a nice girl and cute. Curvy, with wild brown curls and gumball eyes. When crossing paths, she and Jack would often smile hello. And now she goes down into the alley with Gerald Fiorino! Nice, thought Jack, to press a girl like Natalie up against you. Tongue her. Really, though…how could she be with that piece of fucking shit?! Why not just jerk-off a dog, Jill Conklin did.

Mouth agape, squeezing a Spaldeen that he'd previously been bouncing, Jack turned to his equally freaked-out friend Szyk, who stood next to him leaning his backside on a parked car and stabbing Jack's stickball bat into the pavement, and exclaimed, "Oh fuck, Szyk, she's now the 'Kiss of Death'!"

And Fiorino was a dirtbag even by dirtbag standards and word got out.

To Jack's amazement, Natalie became known to all as the Kiss of Death. And proceeded to live up to her new name, fucking, sucking, and drugging, with assorted scumbags before being sent away somewhere by her family. Never again to be seen in the neighborhood, since a few weeks later the family Ragovey (her grandmother) moved out.

It can't be her. Well it could, but for that matter it could be one of a million similar looking girls. Hell, it has been like twenty years. Besides, the wacko eyes on this crazed bitch are like nothing I've ever seen.

136

Looking at him as she chewed her chicken and pork fried rice, he looked into her free floating big brown eyes a moment and it hit him. These gumballs were Natalie Ragovey's, short-circuited!

"I can give you a nice cheap blow job when we're done," she offered.

"No," replied Jack. Wondering why he should even care if it is her.

She persisted, "I'm disease free."

"I'm not afraid of disease," replied Jack dismissively, "though for a while I was afraid of going bald." In a casual manner, he then asked, "What's your name?"

"Gemini," she answered.

"Really!" Jack Barish suddenly demanded.

"All right, Natalia. What the fuck do you care anyway?"

Close enough, thought Jack, before replying condescendingly, "Actually, I don't. I'm just making conversation." For a fleeting moment, he did, however, feel genuinely bad for her. But not as bad as he now felt about this entire random meeting. There was no upside to her. All she did was bring him down. Didn't even pretend to listen to the revelations of Rocky. *Is it my fault this crazy bitch decided to make it with Gerald Fiorino?* She was a piece of shit loser, concluded Jack, irredeemably fucked-up well before he ever saw Rocky. Working himself into a muted rage against the entire pre-Rocky period of his life, which he wished to forget, and *this Natalie creature*, came easily.

Rising to her feet, she said, "I'm gonna use the bathroom. That is, if they let me. You know, there ought to be a law against these chink take-out joints that have tables but don't provide paying customers with toilet facilities."

Sitting there, he considered cutting out. Leave now, he thought, before she reappears. But, an opportunist could very well slip in and snatch her unattended coat from the back of the chair. A minute had quietly passed, so they must have allowed her in back. Despite the vague hatred for her that stirred within him, he didn't wish for *the skank* to end up coatless in the cold winter's night. A couple minutes more, he sat—

"And what's your name?" she asked dreamily hovering over him on her way back to her seat.

"Ger—ald," Jack offered up, darkly self-amused.

Shouting, "HE RAPED ME!!" down she pounced, onto his face, "YOU LOUSY PUNK BASTARD!!" biting and clawing, "YOU—NAMED ME!!" her hands clamped tight onto his ears, "HE RAPED ME!! YOU COULD'VE SAVED ME!!" And before he could overpower her, into his mouth, her tongue, she jammed, deep down—

COMMON GROUND

Like Godzilla vs. King Kong, the clash between Joe Proletariat and his landlord was inevitable. Proletariat (a tightly wound, slightly hunched, medium-sized, fifty-two-year-old bachelor), was a card carrying communist with exceptionally long arms. Aside from his very long arms, which may have been the result of decades of carrying shopping bags filled with used books, he was an ordinary- looking, gray-complexioned, white man.

A lifelong Brooklynite, Proletariat was now living in an apartment at 1606 Purdy Street, in the Parkchester section of the Bronx for one year. He made the move in order to be close to his job reassignment, within the Bureau of Motor Vehicles, at its East Tremont location. The reassignment involved a decent pay raise; and besides, after sixteen years in the same apartment he felt it was time for a change. So Proletariat and a comrade loaded a fairly large rented truck to absolute capacity with his belongings and moved him from his multi-racial Brooklyn neighborhood to one in the Bronx. Proletariat, a tightwad, could've easily afforded to hire movers, but you don't amass over $291,000 in savings from a lifetime in civil service by doing that. Every penny spent was filtered through a hyper-vigilant cash consciousness.

For his political causes, he did good work. Like collecting discarded eye-glass frames from retail optical establishments, for shipment to Cuba. High-end frames, however, he held on to. He went to Nicaragua, and aided the Sandinistas. In Manhattan's Central Park, for himself, he rolled up his sleeves to snatch coins from the bottom of the shallow water of the Bethesda Fountain. Coins tossed for good luck by whimsical pedestrians.

The day Proletariat moved from his Brooklyn apartment, his old landlord was moved to make love to his wife for the first time in fifteen years. Proletariat had made it a point to know all his rights as a tenant. *Landlord.* Even as a kid, he was repulsed by that word. What made some asshole lord of the land? What the fuck was this anyway? Feudalism?

The first seven months at his Bronx apartment all was OK. Heat and hot water. He got to know neighbors. Roaches and occasional mice were of no concern to him. For the first time since the almost decade old collapse of the Soviet Union, a day or two would now sometimes pass without him feeling depressed by it.

He became friendly with a fellow fifty-plus bachelor neighbor. A tall, gaunt, unemployed, Australian expatriate, Kevin Skelly, who, although apolitical, shared his passion for the strictly solo activities of sniffing through every inch of thrift shops and opportunistic street scavenging. Proletariat, for the most part, was able to limit his acquisitions to items he might actually use someday, and those which he deemed valuable. The Aussie was out of control. From old televisions to a prosthetic leg, from floor to ceiling piles of dust smothered books to stacks of wooden orange crates packed with record albums, to his gang of cats, his large apartment was navigable only by moving crabwise and cautiously. When it came to unavoidable retail purchases, they were attitudinal twins. Quantity over quality: single-ply toilet paper, canned corn beef, and plenty of sugar packets with coffee to go.

Proletariat always got a kick out of the Aussie's insane clutter. Seeing it helped him keep his own propensity for it under control, by serving as a reminder of the ultimate clutter horror. He limited his own thrift shop buys and street salvage to things he could rationalize, like a seven rotary phone backup. Anyhow, he genuinely liked the mild-mannered Aussie, and when the landlord moved to evict Skelly, at the behest of three tenants complaining about the stench created by his sixteen cats, Proletariat became incensed. "You *don't* put a guy out on the fucking street!" Loath to take one of his plentiful accumulated days off, he made a pledge to his drooping friend to intervene in the problem if things did not go his way.

The housing court judge ruled to give the Aussie two weeks to get rid of most of the cats, and rectify his odorous living situation. A hearing date was then scheduled for three weeks. In the interim between weeks two and three, a health inspector would make a home visit to the Aussie. Although this seemed fair enough to Proletariat, his hatred for landlords had been triggered. In an even more heightened state of landlord abuse mindfulness than usual, he noticed that the hot water was very hot. Immediately after being turned on. Too damn hot. He would check into it.

At Proletariat's urging, the Aussie got rid of ten of his cats. After making dozens of calls he succeeded in finding new homes for only three. The remaining seven, he took out to Queens, to the shelter at the Center for Animal Care and Control. The volunteer there was a hefty white woman with a mane of wild gray hair and Sixties style, small and circular granny-glasses. She had no sympathy for the heartfelt pain he expressed at being forced to part with the majority of his beloved cats. The cats she regarded lovingly, with a sense of awe. As though each meowing box was a self-consuming burning bush. But, reacted to his profound sadness with disdain. And even though he had handed her a one hundred dollar check, in full payment of her agency fee, she refused to give him a receipt. He wanted the receipt to show the health inspector who would be visiting his apartment. But the events of the day had left him so dejected he meekly departed, perplexed. Clueless, that the divine love this woman displayed for cats was only cover for an even greater passion—hatred of men!

Further urging by Proletariat sparked the Aussie to work diligently in an attempt to clean the entire apartment, working around the awesome clutter as best he could. Skelly became vigilant about keeping the kitty litter-boxes as fresh as possible. Previously, he had indeed been negligent. The future was anyone's guess. Presently, he kept cloying cherry incense burning all day.

Friday of the second week, three days after the health inspector's visit, the Aussie received notice that the apartment *passed* inspection. His relief, however, would be short-lived, because in Monday's mail he received a letter from the court stating that the hearing date, which was for tomorrow, remained in effect. The landlord, now with the aid of a lone tenant and a lawyer on retainer, had persisted in following through with the hearing.

Early that evening the Aussie, appearing strangely calm, almost resigned, informed Proletariat. Figuring that the positive inspection had rendered the hearing moot, Proletariat was shocked and outraged that the landlord was pressing on (even though he knew that the landlord had nothing to lose and plenty to gain). If the landlord could vacate that apartment he could substantially increase the rent. Proletariat assured his friend that he, Joe Proletariat, would join him tomorrow on his behalf as a witness at the hearing. This was war.

That night Proletariat recruited for the cause another loner tenant, Ray Ortiz, with whom he was friendly. The low-key, unionized hospital worker barely knew the Aussie. But after a full hour Proletariat briefing, Ortiz agreed to join with them and appear as a pro-Aussie character witness at tomorrow's Housing Court hearing.

Leaving Ortiz' apartment on the second floor, Proletariat got on the elevator and found himself alone with the sole remaining tenant complainant. An attractive, well-dressed, twenty-something, Hispanic single-mother who lived in a third-floor studio apartment with her little boy. As he entered, she acknowledged him with a polite smile of recognition. "You!" Proletariat declared instantly, "are a disreputable agent of the landlord, who will someday be judged by the highest authority of all, God!" An atheist, Proletariat always enjoyed bringing God into it when arguing morality with anyone he deemed to be a believer.

"Blow me!" she shouted into his face as the elevator stopped at three, perfectly timed, by chance, for her departure.

"Blow me?" he mumbled to himself. "Blow me?" he repeated incredulously. Shutting up into his head with, "Why that little fucking cunt!" Feeling somehow violated, he stomped off, at his floor.

And late that night, still agitated by her words, Proletariat, who usually slept very well, could not fall asleep. Sitting up in bed, he considered getting up to read at his living room desk. He got up and, as was his custom, he nodded over at the life-size wooden Indian that faced him from a far corner of his room—indigenous, loyal, and without maintenance cost.

Once in the living room, Proletariat's mental gears shifted from reading to an even higher mode of comfort—the fellatio-of-self mode of assessing the probable value of recently thrifted or scavenged acquisitions.

On top of the modest armoire that he salvaged while walking through Brooklyn Heights back in 1984, rested two recent acquisitions. One, which was what he correctly believed to be the first English edition (London, 1886) of Dostoyevsky's *Crime and Punishment*. A must sell, since he could not in good conscience keep in his home a book by an author whose politics he considered reactionary. The other, a cut-glass decanter that he bought at a nearby thrift shop for five dollars, because he guessed it was very old and worth ten times that. But guess was all he could do, since, unlike books, which he certainly knew, he knew next to nothing about glass. He took it into the kitchen to admire under the bright kitchen light and was moved to rinse it. Held it under the faucet, turned right to hot, it cracked. Three imperfect lines coming together at a point, like a chicken's foot, only longer. Extremely agitated, Proletariat suffered through a sleepless night. Brain locked on receiving financial compensation for this valuable decanter from the landlord due to the excessively hot water.

At seven-thirty the next morning, sleepless but filled with purpose, Proletariat ran down the building superintendent and insisted he inspect the damage to the decanter. The super accompanied him up to his apartment and witnessed the cracked decanter. Proletariat then had himself a cup of instant coffee, extra heavy on the glommed sugar, before indiscriminately throwing on one of several second-generation sport jackets, and heading out on this drab early March morning, to meet the Aussie and Ortiz. For now, the matter of the damaged decanter had to be put aside. *But, right after the hearing…!*

The grateful Aussie announced that he'd pick up the tab for a cab. Proletariat immediately hailed a gypsy cab. And the three men were transported to the old and very large State Supreme Court building on the Grand Concourse, which overlooked Yankee Stadium.

The assigned hearing chamber was a relatively small, stark room, presided by a fully-robed, elderly black male judge. The sole remaining tenant complainant, the young Hispanic woman who had out scored Proletariat in last night's elevator tell-off, was a no-show. Only the attorney appeared for the landlord. Enormous, baby-faced, and perfectly circular, the attorney's physical appearance amazed Proletariat. Six feet circumference in three-piece pinstripe containment. Proletariat sensed that the judge was perturbed at the attorney for his insistence on pursuing the matter despite the non-appearance of any tenant complainants. A pleasurable realization dawned suddenly on Proletariat—This big circle that was attorney couldn't possibly obtain such oversized clothing for a penny less than retail!

The Aussie, who retained no legal counsel, stammered some, but handled himself pretty well on the stand. He simply was truthful. Ortiz was never called. Feeling very oppressed and pissed off, Proletariat was. The following exchanges between him and the landlord's attorney highlighted his brief appearance on the stand:

"Mr. Proletariat," stated the boyish voiced attorney, "you claim to visit Mr. Skelly regularly in his apartment. I ask you. Is there any trace of foul odor?"

Proletariat responded by fussily removing an asthma inhaler from an inner pocket of his jacket, and using it. Showcasing his particular vulnerability to any cat abundance. In actuality, he had not been bothered by asthma for years. "No," was all he said.

Unfazed, the attorney posed another question: "Is it not possible, Mr. Proletariat, for Mr. Skelly to deposit his cats into closets prior to your arrival?"

"No," replied Proletariat.

"No? Why not?" asked the attorney.

"Kevin Skelly has no phone. All my visits are unannounced," Proletariat replied, feigning aloofness.

"Yet!" snapped the attorney in a tone of triumph, as though Proletariat's last response was what he had anticipated, "these cats may be closeted and would that not, in fact, curtail any odor?"

Proletariat paused. "I don't know," he condescended, "I'm not an expert on permeation of odor through doors." No longer willing or able to veil his contempt, on he spoke, "If you wanna know, why don't you station yourself right outside the closed door to the men's room for awhile and sniff around?"

The judge ruled in favor of the Aussie, who profusely thanked Proletariat and Ortiz. Handshakes completed, each of the three men headed off in separate directions. Proletariat took the subway straight home.

Walking through his front door, he tossed his jacket aside, grabbed the large Yellow Pages directory from a closet, his personal address book from his desk, and started dialing his trusty black rotary phone and sat down to complete the call.

First he called the landlord's office. It was not much past noon, yet there was no pick-up. So he left a short but firm message requesting the landlord, a Hassidic Jew by the name of M.(what the M. stood for nobody knew) Bluefarb, to return his call ASAP.

An hour's worth of phone directory thumbing and calls, revealed that the Department of Housing Preservation and Development was the government agency within whose jurisdiction the too-hot water problem fell. Relentlessly, Proletariat re-dialed that number throughout a half hour of busy signals, finally penetrating the recordings to a live voice. Keeping his balance as he was shuffled around from one person to the next, his tone highly civil, requesting always to be transferred not hung up on, his bureaucratic game plan was intact: To stay on the line until he got someone on the other end whom he could somehow stick to and wear down. And although there was no record of any other 1606 Purdy Ave. tenant complaints to the agency in this regard, he was able to pre-vail upon a soft-spoken bureaucrat, convincing him of the urgency of the situation. "First thing tomorrow," he assured Proletariat, "an inspec-tor will be by." Proletariat then piled two more calls onto the landlord's answering machine, knowing full well that the first message had very likely been received and one or one thousand messages he would not get a call back today.

Next morning just before eight o'clock, while waiting for the inspector, he again called the landlord's office. Much to Proletariat's surprise, "Bluefarb speaking," is what he got on the first ring.

"Bluefarb, this is 1606 Purdy, 5P—Proletariat."

"So," interjected Bluefarb, very calmly, "Mr. Proletariat, what can I do for you?"

"Mr. Bluefarb," stated Proletariat, "I am sure by now you are aware of the damage to my cut-glass decanter, a valuable heirloom of incalculable sentimental worth, which resulted from the hazardous hot water condition here at 1606 Purdy Ave. As a result, I intend on taking a two hundred dollar rent deduction next month. I also intend to notify the proper authorities." Proletariat was pleased with the matter-of-fact tone and content of his delivery. He had, of course, already notified the authorities, and awaited the inspector's arrival even as he spoke.

"You are the only one with such a complaint," replied Bluefarb, sounding puzzled by such an unlikelihood.

"That sir, is beside the point," replied Proletariat, slightly annoyed.

"Why don't you simply turn the cold on first, and adjust?" asked Bluefarb.

"I've been doing it this way my entire life!" Proletariat replied defensively.

"Is it my fault that you can't change a habit?" And with that M. Bluefarb gently hung up on Joe Proletariat.

The Talmudic scholar had landed a forceful blow against the dialectical materialist, and some thirty seconds later Proletariat was still stunned, when the loud ding-dong of his doorbell snapped him out of it. It was the inspector from the Department of Housing Preservation and Development. Using a special thermometer, the inspector recorded the hot water temperature at one hundred ninety degrees Fahrenheit. *Sixty degrees higher than the maximum allowed!* It was a buoyant Proletariat that left for work that morning.

As soon as he sat down at his desk, he pushed all job related business aside and hurriedly wrote a letter to Bluefarb. After a very early lunch break, walked over to the Post Office and bought a stamp. Having affixed the stamp to the sealed envelope, he self-satisfiedly dropped it into the appropriate mail slot. Ordinarily, he'd have waited till the end of the work day (as he always did with all his personal mail), in order to slip it, undetected, through the office postage meter. However, this particular matter so pressed on him that he could not hold off taking care of it for even a minute longer. The letter read as follows:

March 14, 2002

Dear Mr. Bluefarb:

A senior inspector from the Department of Housing Preservation and Development was here, in my apartment. He substantiated my claim about the hazardous hot water. You will be hearing from them. There are also many other housing and health code violations here at 1606 Purdy Avenue, such as a roach infestation in the basement and near the openings to the incinerators. I will be reporting this to the proper New York City agencies after giving you proper due warning. When I moved to 1606 Purdy Avenue I expected and wanted to live a quiet and tranquil life. However, due to your insolence and greed this has not been possible. With his own eyes your building superintendent witnessed the destruction from scalding (near the boiling point) water of a priceless decanter which belonged to my great-grandmother. After several unanswered calls to your office I had to report this dangerous problem to the proper city agency. You'll have to have this fixed! This is a serious problem which could result in the scalding of human flesh belonging especially to children and senior citizens. I hereby request you call me at home any morning within ten days of the date of this letter, before eight-thirty at (718) 654-4566 to discuss compensation for my destroyed heirloom. In the interest of expediency I will accept two hundred dollars to put this loss behind me. I will not allow you to harass me or my fellow tenants, like when you heinously attempted to evict my friend Kevin Skelly on spurious grounds and lost out in court. Someday, as all of us will, you too will be judged by the highest authority of all: God Himself!

> Sincerely Yours,
> Joe Proletariat

cc: files

Two days later, as he walked out of his front door for work that morning, Proletariat's phone rang. In he rushed and on the lull following ring two grabbed it, "HEL—LO!" "Is that you, Proletariat?" asked Bluefarb.

"Yes."

"This is Mr. Bluefarb. Listen, I'm willing to do something for you Mr. Proletariat, but I cannot accept any responsibility on your loss. And you've got to behave yourself.

"Behave myself?" Proletariat echoed incredulously, realizing full well that was not possible.

"You can deduct twenty-five dollars from next month's rent, and an additional twenty-five the following month, for a total of fifty dollars," said Bluefarb.

Remarkably, this amount coincided perfectly with the ten times the purchase price formula Proletariat contrived to assess the decanter when he purchased it. And before Proletariat could utter a word, Bluefarb emphatically added, "Look, we both *know* that eighty-five percent of life is money."

"It's a deal," replied Proletariat, finding himself intuitively in total agreement with this precise money/life calculation. A calculation he himself had never consciously explored.

How would each man break down the remaining fifteen percent? Nobody knows.

GODFATHER DEATH

Based on the brothers Grimm fairy tale.

All the days and all the nights, a poor man slaved to feed all his little ones. But when the thirteenth was born, he cried. Not enough hours in the day to earn for another one. So he took off down the road to find a godfather for the boy. A road one goes alone.

Like a foot soldier, he marched. On and on…night was empty as death. Then streaks of silver crossed the dark sky and the sickle moon turned shocking blue—and a beat up old Honda Civic cutoff his path. No driver! Through a crack in the muffler thundered an otherworldly command: "I AM GOD AND I WILL WATCH OVER YOUR SON AND HE WILL THRIVE!"

"If I were you," replied the poor man flatly, "I too, would be ashamed to show my face." And the poor man marched on, wondering why God chose to project from inside the muffler. Why not through the exhaust pipe? It would seem to make more sense. Many miles later he stopped, and urinated into some bushes…

Speckled with droplets, a five-and-a-half-foot-long, fat, scaly, red serpent with a man-shaped head slithered forth from beneath the freshly drenched bush. The serpent rose. Its head was that of a man, its face that of a very ordinary middle-aged man.

"I'm sorry!" exclaimed the poor man.

"Don't sweat it. I lay in wait for you but fell asleep. Lucky for your son, the golden shower woke me. For I am the devil, and I will watch over your son and he will thrive. He will fuck anything that moves and die with the most toys."

"Fucking anything that moves," replied the poor man. "Well, I don't know about that, but I certainly don't believe whoever dies with the most toys wins."

And he marched on and on . . .

Towards a loner who marched towards him. Bones on bones. A skeleton. Clickety-clack-click. Death had come to pitch. "I am Death and I will watch o—"

"Yes!" interrupted the poor man. "Yes! Everybody dies. Homer died. Dante died. Madonna will die."

Godfather Death watched over the boy. He became a great doctor. One who could cure the gravely ill. For Godfather Death had provided him with an occult potion. A universal cure. Along with conditions. If the rattling skeletal hand of his godfather appeared above the head of the bedridden—the potion should be given. If it appeared at the foot of the bed—Classic Coke should be given. Godfather Death graciously allowed a fifty-fifty live or die split. And advised his godson never to disobey the conditions, because the punishment would be his life.

The great doctor lacked for nothing. Cash and classy ladies in abundance. Yet he always made time to aid the poor. So when a musty old woman hunched over an empty shopping cart knocked on his door, and begged him to make a house call to her dying 17-year-old granddaughter, he hailed a cab and off they went.

The ridged contours of the drab woolen blanket that the doctor looked down upon hid the frail girl under it. Only honey-colored hair and a small chalky forehead were uncovered. From beneath the blanket came her muffled song—a lullaby. And it thrilled him. Thrilled him to tears. She, he resolved instantly, would be his wife. But the rattling skeletal hand appeared at the foot of her bed. Quickly he tore off the blanket, and spun her like a bottle. The skeletal hand now appeared above her head. And he gave her the potion . . .

Godfather Death summoned him. Ordered his godson the doctor to meet him way down an abandoned coal mine in Boone County, West Virginia. There stood Godfather Death. Amid a deep circle of flickering candles. Perfect posture. Arms crossed. A big-boned son of a gun.

"It won't happen again," said his godson.

"Especially not if you're dead," replied Godfather Death. He then posed a question to him. "Godson, if you had to choose between remaining the great doctor I made you or making this girl your wife—which would you choose?"

"The girl," replied the godson.

"That is the better choice," said Godfather Death. "But if I were you, I wouldn't make any plans beyond exactly two years and one minute from right now…"

Scapegoat

The team of fifteen-year-old softballers taking the field of cement that July afternoon, for an unorganized schoolyard contest at P.S.105 in the Bronx, was not a good one. Our first baseman, Rob Warren, was a jump-shooting basketball phenom. Irving from Texas, our shortstop, was a quick-fisted, manly, cross between Joe Namath and Elvis, and a consummate "getter" of girls. But good softball players, not one. No spastics, just unskilled and undisciplined.

I was in my head at second base, brain locked on "Hello Goodbye" by the Beatles: "'hello, hello / I don't know why you say goodbye / I say hello / hello, hello / I don't know why you say goodbye / I say hello ...'"

I don't think we had a right fielder, and the "official pitcher" (one who pitches to both sides) was a hulking seventeen-year-old, red-headed tomboy—Gilda. She also served as the lone umpire. A good ball-player, she was looking for a guy to play stickball against when we drafted her. She agreed because she got to hone her pitching skills, and be at the center of the action.

At third base was barrel-chested pinhead "Little Rosie," Jeff Rosenblatt. He had an older pot dealing brother, Fred, who at 5'6" and close to three-hundred pounds was "Big Rosie."

Big Rosie dealt quantity. He was partners in pot dealing with their father. They kept fifteen-hundred dollars operating cash stashed underneath a floorboard in the foyer of their apartment.

Last summer, as fire raged through their building, Big Rosie and the father stood outside the evacuated building FREAKING about the cash. The firefighters held their own battling the fire. Two minutes later Little Rosie showed up, to eat. His father and big brother quickly convinced him to mad dash into the burning building to fetch the cash. He did, and he rescued the cash. Some boys laughed in his face over that. Others, behind his back.

Catching was a profanity-spewing fire hydrant named Eugene, who by inserting two fingers into his mouth could produce an ear-quaking whistle. He could also "clam" at will. That is, sounding like an air gun, he'd expectorate a glob of clammy missile. In center was some kid Irv grabbed off the street. And in left, was a favorite target of every bully— Neil Fogelfish. A fair sized boy who got "beat on" regularly because he did not retaliate. He was—"Feesh."

The opposing team was a bunch from across the Bruckner Expressway. I didn't know any of them. They appeared to be around our age but did not go to the same school as us. A couple of our guys seemed to know a couple of their guys. Which is probably how the game came together. What I did know, after two innings, was that they were no better than us.

In the top of the third we're ahead 4-3, but with one out, they load the bases. The batter hits a high hopper to short that our third baseman Little Rosie manages to cut-off and flip to me at second for one and I fire to first where Rob Warren stretches like a major leaguer to scoop up my low hard throw. This miraculously executed double play splendor would have ended the inning, but Gilda called the close play at first in favor of the runner. Her call was correct. As Rob was getting to his feet one run had already scored, knotting it at 4, and their three base runners were buffalo STAMPEDING around the base paths. In an attempt to head off the go ahead run, he unleashed a furious throw in the general direction of home plate that hit the runner heading home in the head with a THUD collapsing him like a sack of bricks and triggering our team collective unconscious.

Led by the left side of our infield, we rushed out to left field—to beat on Feesh—who earlier in the game had committed an inconsequential error. GAME OVER.

On Maxie Off

The Background

Some people have no sense of time. Such a person was Maxie Pomerantz. He was ALWAYS late. That's if he showed up at all. As a result of this personality trait, at around thirteen years of age he became known in our Bronx neighborhood as "Maxie Off." Or simply—"Off." Years later, a local drug-dealer theorized that a piece of Maxie's brain had to be missing. But I knew better. His brain was cool. He just didn't give a fuck about what time it was. Never did. Whatever he was doing: smoking weed, scheming, handicapping the ponies, or sleeping—he'd be totally into it. Nothing else mattered. His existence transcended the ordinariness of time. He had innate intelligence and a good heart. But an inability to do an HONEST days work. It was impossible for him. More on that later. The first time I met him—

I was seated toward the front of the classroom in seventh-grade, on the first day of the 1971 school year, as the teacher, Mr. Howser, sternly addressed us hushed students. He was feeling us out, and we were feeling him out. From the back of the class I hear—

HA!

HA!!

HA!

Three loud unrestrained mono-syllabic blasts of laughter—the second the loudest.

I turn around. It was this kid Maxie Pomerantz, laughing openly—in the teacher's face. Over who knows what?

He was told to shut up, and two laugh blasts later, he did.

After I got to know Maxie, I came to realize that he wasn't trying to show the teacher up. He just laughed, heartily, whenever—the fuck— he found something funny, and didn't CARE to know better.

Long as I knew him, the ten years to follow, this did not change. Nor did any of the aforementioned features of his personality ever change. This combination of qualities propelled him to legendary exploits. As these exploits mounted, his name further evolved and split off into the more formal—"the Officer." "The Officer" could be used interchangeably with "Off" or "Maxie Off." Depending on one's arbitrary impulse, at any moment in time.

The Root of Pathology

Six-two and about 200 lbs. at twenty-two, the Officer was an imposing guy. He had green eyes and thick, wavy black hair. But, his head was too small for his body, his complexion sallow, and his hips too wide for his shoulders. Nevertheless, he could dunk a basketball.

Since his conviction the year before (on a felony to which he pleaded guilty and got five years probation), he seemed much older. Although, I could not put my finger on what it was about him that changed. Maybe I changed.

He loved a buck. That could NEVER change. He HAD TO have it. Had to have it for gambling, drugs, gas, and girls. But, he did not like work. When it came to making a buck he HAD TO detour at the law, or break it.

So, he and I are sitting on the dirty green carpeted floor in his room, upstairs in his parents' very modest Bronx home. A home he had yet to move from. Sitting around smoking pot and Marlboros, watching the Knicks play the 76ers on channel 9, in 1981. We needed Knicks. I was down for fifty bucks. Phoned it into a bookie.

Maxie Off's credit was no good, anywhere. But, since he made big punches—five hundred bucks a pop—one bookie, hungry for Off's action, would dispatch one of his long-ago broken losers, as a footman, to meet Off and get cash—up front.

I was already high on Seconal. We took hits of his mediocre coke intermittently. The game was tight and the dark smoky room our clearly defined world. We needed Knicks. No knock—the door swings open. A bare flabby arm of a woman—BANANA—held in hand—is all that enters—a bare flabby arm of a woman—BANANA—held in hand—"Maxie, *nem** a banana!" The voice—his Polish Jewish mother, presenting her Maxala—A PERFECT YELLOW BANANA!

The Deeds

The window in the men's room at the Howard Johnson—across from the Bronx Zoo on Southern Boulevard—could be slid up no more than a foot. So, in order for Off to get each five-gallon cardboard cylinder—containing ice cream—out through the window, he had to position them horizontally, before dropping them into the back alley. Where he'd go collect them after punching out on Sundays when his shift—bussing tables—was done for the day. Off would then carry the ice-cold containers down the block and around the corner to a local luncheon-

---

* Yiddish - *take*

ette, where they were very happy to get Howard Johnson ice-cream, real cheap.

The job at Howard Johnson also required him to fill-in as cashier. Off mastered the cash register, and the opportunities it afforded him— to steal, real quick. The cash register became his "piano" and he, a virtuoso. It was a talent which served him well, in all future employment, where he was called upon to cashier.

That was Maxie Off's first job—after turning sixteen—and getting his working papers. He had no vices to support—yet. Nor, did he lack for anything at home. Off figured, "Everybody steals." And, "Fuck those Jew-haters, anyway." Two elements which, in combination with one another, produce one powerfully compounded solid position.

XXXXXXXXXX

Off had only a learner's permit to drive when the tall seventeen-year-old somehow managed to get hired as deliveryman for Blue-Star Kosher Butchers. He was to drive their van, delivering orders of meat to customers, and collecting payment for these meats. He did. He also smuggled meat out of the store and sold it. And regularly fleeced Blue-Star of cash, sharply maneuvering, as handler of their cash. He figured, "Fuck those cheap Jews."

At night he'd steal the van and shoot up to Yonkers Raceway. He was hooked on horses. Smoked a loose one and shot his nuts playing ponies.

As with every job he ever had, after a few months, he was fired. Even when Maxie Off had a real good thing, his lateness was certain. As certain as the sunrise.

At eighteen, he got his driver's license. Within months, he was blacklisted by every yellow cab company in Manhattan. He'd show up late, work a few hours, take the cab to the track, get "robbed" and return the cab—empty-handed. Sometimes, right before returning the cab, he'd report the "robbery" to the local police precinct where he "got robbed."

A year later, Off bought a used two-door, red, black-top, fastback Cutlass. A sharp car, never to be washed again. We could now shoot to Roosevelt Raceway out on Long Island. Crossing the Whitestone Bridge, we'd look for an unblocked, out-of-operation automated tollbooth, whose wooden arm—that was supposed to be down—was in the up position. Conditioned drivers would stop their cars by the metal basket and mindlessly drop their coins into it. We'd go right through—never paying. Maxie Off spotted this—instantly—for the set-up that it was.

Unaccounted monies collected, to be split-up among "the boys" working that shift.

Sometimes, coming back, if no toll was set-up for the boys, the Officer would drive right through a manned booth, slapping his empty hand hard against the toll collector's open palm—

HA!

HA!!

HA!

Done—and never caught. After we won at the track or lost.

xxxxxxxxxx

Never a lucky gambler, he was a good handicapper. And, for a week or two, could get very hot. During these scientifically (as opposed to luck) fueled hot streaks, I only had to reach into my pocket to cover my own bets. Diner costs, track admissions and programs, bar tabs and pot, he covered. But money in his pocket did not mean payment for his creditors. Unless, he was confronted with imminent physical danger by capable bone-breakers, he wasn't paying anyone.

One winning night, we're up in the clubhouse at Yonkers Raceway, and on this Saturday night even the clubhouse is packed. We're standing underneath one of the televised tote boards, smoking, handicapping, and occasionally looking up at the televised tote board, when a cologne-soaked, rhino-necked enforcer spots the Officer for someone, who he believes, has reneged on a couple hundred owed the storefront bookie joint, where the enforcer was one of several clerks. He believed right.

He comes over to where we're standing, "I know you!" he accusingly says to the Officer, as though the Officer was disguised as a tea-kettle, but couldn't fool him—his left index finger in Off's chest—

"WHAT'RE—YOU—SOME KIND OF HOMO?!" The Officer shouts into his face—and the eyes of the crowd of gamblers—some with girlfriends—fix upon a—now—confused and self-conscious enforcer—who slinks away shaking his head left to right to left . . .

The unshakable Officer sensed some uncertainty, and so, the cologne-soaked, rhino-necked enforcer was victimized by the master of reversion. He was not the first such victim, nor would he be the last.

xxxxxxxxxx

I unloaded the last of the truckload of large cartons, that had previously been packed by Off with one hundred small boxes of Kotex sanitary napkins per carton, off of Off's rented truck. The owner of the South Bronx drug store, in front of which we were double-parked, was now doing a quick count of them as Off hovered over his back, bombing the bald top of the old druggist's radish-like head with bluish cigarette smoke exhalations. That each small sample box had imprinted on it SAMPLE—NOT FOR SALE mattered not, to the owner of drug stores. Grinning a self-congratulatory grin, he handed the Officer crisp cash, and we were gone.

This caper was made possible when a prominent marketing firm hired the Officer to manage a short-term project for them. He was to supervise the distribution of small sample boxes of Kotex sanitary napkins, throughout a slice of Westchester. They never bothered to check Off's fraudulent resumé. He, being naturally delusional, believed it. Why shouldn't they?

Not only were no samples distributed to the public, but also the entire amount allocated for payroll was paid to himself, under several aliases—and me. He was a generous guy. I got several paychecks for doing nothing, and I didn't even have to kickback. Over the next couple of days most all the money made from the Kotex sample box sale was "donated" to the track.

XXXXXXXXXX

No regulars at the track are winners. None. Losers all. The "game" grinds you into dust. With only loose change left between the two of us, after, another losing night, and the fuel indicator well below E, we were feeling very lucky just to make it back to the Bronx. Suddenly—a big black Buick Wildcat cuts us off—screeching smokily—to a stop—causing the Officer to slam the brakes on the Cutlass—bringing us to a similarly abrupt rubber-burning stop. The big black Wildcat is known to us—

A loose-built, long-haired giant emerges, in sections, from the driver's side. A regular-sized guy, wiry and blond, has jumped out the other side. The big guy is the Big Bluff, named in dishonor of his crappy poker game, and the other, cocksman turned junkie—Silverman. Tight-fisted, glowers pasted—the duo approaches. We've remained seated as they position themselves, one at each of our doors. The Big Bluff—the loose-built, long-haired giant by Off's door. And his smack-commando—Silverman—by mine.

"You got till Thursday to pay up!" Is the Bluff's ultimatum to the Officer, an ultimatum issued by the deep-toking marijuana marathoner through orthodontically adjusted horsy choppers—

HA!

HA!!

HA!

The Officer laughs right in his face.

Muttering—bloody Thursday threats—the Big Bluff and Silverman hop back into the Wildcat, and tear off under the El.

Apparently, Maxie Off buying the Big Bluff all the cereal he could eat, and then turning him on to super-potent sweet black opiated hash panacea, after the Bluff's parents threw their son out of the house last year, didn't count for much anymore to the towering former poker player, forever pot glutton—

HA!

HA!!

HA!

I couldn't stop laughing either.

xxxxxxxxxx

The Officer took a civil service test, scored on top, presented well at the interview, and was hired: by the New York State Dept. of Taxation and Finance—as a Tax-Compliance Agent. There couldn't have been much of a background check done. If there had been, several misdemeanor convictions would have been discovered. Just one month prior, he was arrested when police raided an abandoned Spanish Harlem building, where he was one of eighty-seven men arrested, betting on live dog-fights.

As a Tax-Compliance Agent, the twenty-year-old Maxie Off, was to visit businesses that were tax delinquent and effect collection. He had the power to seize bank accounts and shutdown businesses. On the days he was required to work in the office, he'd show-up late. As a result, he became the first and only agent ever to have to punch-in on the clock. This had no affect on his lateness.

However, when he was out in the field and actually worked, this bettor of horses, ballgames and dogs, would astound his supervisor with superior productivity. This, in spite of the fact that much of the time he was supposed to be out in the field working, he'd be home, asleep. He had added a new quinella to his repertoire: cocaine and girls.

Deeply seasoned in deceit, he was shy and green when it came to girls. He had yet to learn that girls did not have to be an expense. Gambling, drugs, and girls: a breakneck action box for the Officer.

Lots of cash was needed, for him to carry on. He began shaking-down tax debtors. Some, who knew they were being shook-down.

Others, who knew they were being shook-down, but didn't want to know. And one who didn't even know he was being shook-down. In every case, cash to the Officer was cheaper than checks to the government. And the Officer mastered the art of the shakedown. However, his breakneck action box proved to be a natural disaster so ravenous, it overwhelmed even his artistry. He ended up copping a plea to a felony (the same felony mentioned earlier) and was sentenced to the five years probation and a $5,000 fine.

He spent the next several months amassing the cash, by dealing large amounts of Quaaludes he'd acquired from an acquaintance who was a pharmacist. The pharmacist was under pressure to support his wife and two children in a comfortable lifestyle. The Officer was under pressure to gamble, get high, and make payments on the fine. He did, however, get himself a couple low-maintenance girlfriends.

Epilogue

That was then. Today, the thirty-eight-year-old Officer lives in New Jersey with his wife Laura and their two children. They've been married for close to twelve years. The marriage has had some rocky spots, but they've always stayed together. He's toned down his gambling and only smokes pot.

Their two children, Larry (10 years old), and Cara (8), are adorable and appear to be doing well. Although, some say that the Officer puts undue pressure on skilled little Larry, drilling into the psyche of his young son Off's own living adolescent Yankee fantasy. His wife Laura runs her own small business, a local daycare center. Assisted by her staff of one, she handles everything. Her workday is long and exhausting.

The Officer works part-time, but earns more. He sells ad-space in community-watch newspapers that he publishes. This is his fifth year in this business. His is a one man operation. He is very adept at enabling potential customers to exhibit their civic responsibility, by kicking-in to support their community-watch paper. His unflappability, resolve and resourcefulness, combine to make his pitch a kind of customized voodoo. His success rate selling space to immigrant owners of retail establishments is exceptionally good. He regularly acquires new accounts, and although none of his customers have ever seen the ads they've paid for, many continue to advertise regularly. Actually, no one has ever seen any of the papers he publishes. Not even he.

156

Me, The Psychic Space Eater, and the Speech Therapist

He was a psychic space eater. From 50 feet, I could sense this about the bulky old man walking steadily down the block in the direction of the Second Avenue bus stop, where only I waited. Heavy presence. A type of person who simply cannot blend in, has to get noticed. Annoying, but basically harmless. On this cold, January day in Manhattan, his hands were buried in the pockets of his rumpled, putrescent-brown-colored, ankle-length raincoat. Some 20 feet from me, he came to a complete halt alongside a large, sitting, white mutt and its owner, a young woman in a long down coat and hood.

Broad faced, thick lipped, and bushy browed: Russian? His was the face of a genius or a fool. The odds did not favor the former. The stocking cap he wore was the same putrescent-brown as his raincoat. An impossible match. Maybe, he was a genius. He turned slightly left, looked down at the mutt, and beamed a grotesque, blissful smile at it. He seemed awestruck, smiling on, for 30 solid seconds, as though he were an ancient Hebrew witnessing the parting of the Red Sea. Still smiling that smile, he turned to face the mutt's owner. Blankly, she looked right through him. Brutal. Completely ignored him. Smiling no longer, he turned away.

He then approached the bus stop where I stood. A congregation of horseflies hovered just above of his head. As he drew closer, however, I could see that the horsefly congregation was actually extensive pilling from his stocking cap. At that moment the bus pulled up. And although I look through no one, I was very pleased not to have to deal with whatever he would inevitably have dealt. Especially, since a recent surgery left my right vocal cord paralyzed, rendering my voice an exhausting, breathy whisper. Naturally, he cut ahead of me and took an excessive amount of time to produce and swipe his MetroCard, and move on, blocking my entrance and keeping me out in the cold.

It was late morning and the bus mostly vacant. I walked to the middle, and before taking a seat, watched as he plopped into one of the seats up front by the driver. Only then did I take a left-side window seat. Four local stops and I get off. Nevertheless, I loosened my scarf and removed my Mets cap. First stop, 91st Street. Only one man boarded and took a seat in the rear. As the bus pulled out, the old psychic space eater rose to his feet and turned to the aisle. Staggering stiffly, sleepwalker-like, down the aisle of the moving bus, he came, this Frankenstein monster. Passing nothing but vacant seats, he plopped into the one right next to me. Like a jack-in-the-box, I popped up, and without so much as a glance moved to the back of the bus.

No energy for him. He remained seated.

At the 86th St. stop he again rose, and moved back to his original seat up front. I glanced out the window, focusing solely on storefront signs: Imperial Cleaners, Señor Swanky's, Serenity Nail Spa....Next stop, 79th Street, he got off. Because I was seated on the other side of the bus and chose to remain seated, I could not observe him from a window. At 72nd Street, I got off. And in less time than it takes to milk a cow, I was in the speech therapist's modest office for my second visit. On opposite sides of what looked to be a children's finger-painting table, she and I sat. Face to face.

Caroline Bell was an attractive, fortyish, mid-western blonde. Pale blue eyes and remarkably smooth skin. More importantly, she was competent and caring. She spoke unaffected American in a girlish voice. The quality of which was well represented by her last name. A voice of which I can't ever imagine tiring of. She asked me if I had practiced the exercises at home. Exercises like the one with which we would soon begin—while pressing my palms together and turning head left, rasping "E-e-e-e-e" 3 times, with breaths in between. I nodded affirmatively. A total lie. Once I found out the work I was doing with her was intended to make things more bearable for now, but had no restorative effect on the paralyzed vocal cord, I didn't even bother. She demonstrated a vocal exercise. I repeated it: Exercise after exercise. From across the small table, she kept her eyes on me. I began to feel special, like a little boy who is the sole object of his lovely kindergarten teacher's attention. She paused to ask me what I was doing for the scar on my neck. Mutely, I held my palms up and casually shrugged as if to say, Huh, what am I supposed to be doing? "Cocoa butter in slow circular motions," she replied. "Slow circular motions." She was concerned with the corrugated garter snake of a scar across my neck. I was not. So what if it looked as though my neck had been opened using a beer can opener? I was solely concerned with coming out on the right side of the 50/50 odds of my voice returning. That left no one to be concerned about the next phase of the cancer treatment.

I must've just missed the bus at 72nd Street, because there was no one waiting. Preferring not to remain standing in the cold, I lowered my head and, leaning slightly forward, put one foot in front of the other, weaving through the human traffic at a deliberate pace. Not nearly recovered from the neck surgery, by 77th I was tired and bone-chilled. Slipped into a Rite Aid pharmacy, just long enough to warm and recharge. And out. When I reached 79th, I spotted the bus up ahead idling at the stop. Ran. Caught it. Huffing, puffing, and pleased with myself as I swiped my Metrocard and turned: There he was! Sitting right before my eyes—in the bank of seats closest to the driver, facing the entrance. Face and torso covered by the newsprint tent that was the unfurled New York Times, he, ostensibly, was reading. The one-of-a-kind putrescent-brown-colored ankle-length coat. The old psychic space eater! Taking up three seats though, officially, his bottom occupied only one forcing anyone who wishes to sit there to engage him. Refusing to prolong fate's little joke, I hotfooted it to the middle of the bus, and an instant before the bus pulled out, managed to exit.

Having absorbed the cost of bus fare, I now decided to splurge. Dove straight into a cab. Twelve blocks in no time. Handed the driver a $5 bill, buck tip, and told him to keep the change. Decompressing, I began walking the short distance into the lobby of my building. Glanced down at a medium sized, standing, black mutt. Brought a smile to my face. Looked up at its lolling owner, and smiled at the furry-earmuffed, bright-brown-eyed young woman. Blankly, she looked right through me. I quickly turned away and walked on through the revolving door.

ONCE UPON A DREAM

Yes, that's what she said. I was quite certain. "He's not right—in the head." About me, I heard all right, all right. To our mutual neighbor, in the hallway, as I turned the key to open my ground floor apartment door. A woman of about a hundred years, slumped over her walker, said that to another lady of at least eighty.

Why? Because I have not spoken to any of the other tenants in this three floor urban walk-up in the eleven years I've lived here? Or, maybe because they hear me coming or going in the middle of the night? I do nod hello. Well, let them say what they will. I do not want to—ever—have to engage in small talk with any of them.

Inside, I turn the lock shut. Who am I? I'm a man like any other man. More so in some ways, less in others. I drink more coffee but I bed less women. A middle-aged civil servant, I am ordinary-looking and I pay my bills on time. Perfectly fit and unattached. I undress and hit the sack.

In bed, I lie on my back and replay my flirtation with the new waitress in the Rainbow. Suzie. As usual, I ate supper at the Rainbow Diner. Right after she took my order, before I could conjure up a case against her, I introduced myself. Our eyes locked steady. "I'm Suzie," she then declared, breaking the spell. She smiled sweetly. Pretty Suzie, of fair complexion and shoulder-length, straight, light-brown hair, back in a ponytail. The short shiny black skirt she wore wrapped nice on her rounded behind. Discreetly, I continued to feast an eye upon her... When she served my coffee and burger-deluxe (includes fries and a tiny paper cup of coleslaw), I smiled. And ate . . .

Meal devoured, I placed two dollars under the empty cup and headed up to the counter to pay. Despite an electrical current of intestinal anxiety, I forced myself to detour four steps, to Suzie, who was busy serving a table of two. Said, "Good night."

As she whisked by, she affectionately tapped my left elbow with her free hand and replied, "G'night."

Tomorrow, or the day after, I will do it. I'll ask Suzie out. No later. No matter what. Well all right! Now, home for some rest.

After my usual four fitful hours of dreamless sleep I awoke. Shaken and stiff. It was 2:00 AM. I knew I would not be able to fall back asleep for at least an hour. So, I got up. Pissed, dressed, and went out to walk.

It was warm for a late October night and my light sweatshirt felt just right. Walking provided relief. I walked along Center Street, for some ten minutes, passing the gated storefronts and a few other solitary men in drift, when my mellowing mood was badly jarred. Led Zeppelin's over overblown, existential bubblegum rock-anthem "Stairway to Heaven" BOOMED from a passing van SO LOUD my internal organs—almost—burst. To escape, and lessen exposure to passing cars, I spurted ten or so yards to the corner, by the twenty-four hour Shell station, and turned left down a residential street.

Less than a quarter of a block in front of me, on the same side of the sleeping, tree-lined street, I could see the backs of a couple leisurely walking side by side. The trim girl wore white jeans. I'd bet on a pretty girl. Very pretty. Her partner was a medium-sized guy. Short hair and a sweatshirt. From the back, he could be me.

I sped up my pace and closed the gap, but made sure not to get close enough for them to hear my steps. I had a thousand eyes—I had nothing better to do.

Well before the end of the long block, by the driver side of a parked car, they stopped and talked.

I stepped into the dimly lit doorway of a small apartment building, from where I'd be able to continue to spy on them. Suddenly, a woman popped out from behind the other side of the car and joined the guy—in PUMMELING the girl in white jeans. All appeared blurry. The pummel momentum very quickly landed the girl on her back—on the hood of the car. The female half of the assault duo then paused and poked her partner on his shoulder. She pointed across the street. At a laughing man, who was looking back at them and holding up a video camera. He had all of it on tape! Me too? My cowardice would be exposed! Or worse, I'll be indicted as an accomplice! I turned and walked away, briskly. Like an assassin, fleeing the scene of his hit.

It was a quarter of three when I entered my apartment. Collapsing onto the loveseat in my living room. I had purchased the brown leather loveseat this past year. It was very comfortable.

A state employee for close to fifteen years—I process food stamp applications—I decided to spend some savings on new furnishings. Modest, but new. The place was now female-company friendly. I even painted. The walls however remain undecorated.

But the ugly business of tonight has ruined everything. In this very loveseat, I had hoped to sit, with Suzie, and chat intimately. Our fine conversation intermingling with the exquisite sounds of Brahms' intermezzos would scrub the air. Ah, but what will she think of me now? And what will the old bats whisper?

Two hours chewed a deep tunnel of blue doom through my head, before I realized that I was guilty—of nothing. And anyway, if accused,

I will deny—deny—deny. Even if I am presented with my own image on video, I will deny that it is me.

When the Saturday morning sun rose I laid down to sleep. I imagined that old bat whispering, "He's not right—in the head," about me, and proceeded to tighten the muscles of my right thigh, in order to change the channel in my head, to sweet thoughts of Suzie—before falling asleep.

Warm, soft hands caressed my stubbled face.

"Those hands feel good," I said.

"They are good," replied Suzie.

Opening my eyes, I knew it was way past noon.

I made a pot of coffee, and remained standing by the kitchen counter as I drank a cup. I figured I'd do some light cleaning around the apartment. But instead, I left the shades drawn over all the windows and went into the living room. Flicked on the TV. And sat in my loveseat.

I kept the sound off, and watched an attractive red-headed girl-next-door type, in a navy-blue jacket, begin to deliver the news. There was a knock on the door to my apartment. When I got there, no one was there. Perhaps that was a cryptic message from the laughing man with the tape! No, I consoled myself, I was simply—just hearing things.

On TV the same woman newscaster seamlessly shifted her expression back and forth from a smile to seriousness. Now and then, she'd slightly tilt her head left, alluringly. Less often, flashing her bare right palm. It was we two. And finally, craning her neck for exclamatory purposes. Why, she could have been reporting on anything, from world hunger to Courtney Love!

In the shower I soaped up heavily. Finished showering. I toweled myself dry and combed my hair. Taking more time than usual to shave, I successfully avoided nicks.

After changing into fresh Fruit of the Looms and getting a refill of coffee, I went into the living room and put on a CD. The songs of early country blues artist—Blind Willie McTell.

Feel like a broke down engine ain't got no drivin' wheel... His vocals and guitar strumming, however, rose joyfully above the pained words. Sitting in my loveseat, head bopped to rhythm, gently. *I went down to my prayin' ground and fell on bended knees . . .*

I remained seated, when the music ended. Eyes open or shut, mind's grainy image of Suzie...fell apart. But the shadow of love strengthened my heart.

Locked on my—make a date with Suzie—mission, it was 6:00 PM when I left my apartment for the direct to Rainbow ten minute walk.

The Rainbow was packed but I couldn't wait. Inside, I stood in front by the cashier and scanned the floor for Suzie. Since there was only one dining room—and it was brightly lit—this wasn't difficult.

I needed to see if she was working. In no more than half a minute, I spotted her as she emerged from the back of the room. She had gotten a short haircut!

Balancing a tray of food on her left shoulder and palm, she was coming from the pick-up area of the kitchen. The short haircut looked cute on her. She'd no longer have to wear her hair back while working. From where I stood, Suzie actually looked trimmer than she did yesterday. Different. No matter. She looked mighty good last night and she looks mighty good tonight. Although her station was full, she glanced my way and appeared to notice me. How would it look if I left now, only to come back and sit in her station? Shamefully transparent!

Because I was alone, the owner, an easy going Greek named George, who also served as host, politely motioned me over to the counter.

The layout at the Rainbow was standard. A long counter, where customers dined sitting on swivel stools, ran parallel to four rows of connected family-sized booths. The rows were separated by aisles. The only unusual thing about the entire diner was the very large color portrait of George Washington which hung prominently on the far wall.

Part of the station Suzie worked tonight was in the first aisle. Right behind my seat! All I had to do was turn around. I may not be able to make my move, but I will reinforce our relationship.

Not too bad, except I was hemmed in at the counter. At my left elbow was a pock-marked, pot-bellied, old ashtray that was a man choking a racing form and grumbling about cold coffee and a fixed race. And at my right elbow was a bearish, blond-bearded, young man in a filthy red down-vest. He was reading a book, which he held, eye-level, in his left hand. All the text had been highlighted in orange or green. The book had to do with quantum theory. Couldn't I at least have a polished little lady on one side of me?

I ordered my usual coffee and burger-deluxe from the Mexican counterman. He was all business. Over my left shoulder, I looked upon Suzie, as she worked the tables on the other side of the aisle. I wanted, merely, to make eye-contact and smile hello. She was being coy. I'd have to wait until she was right before me and say hello. I didn't have to wait long.

I was turned fully around, watching her, as she stepped over to wait on the table in front of me. For a moment, we were face to face.

And I called her name, "Hi Suzie!" When she did not instantly reply, I repeated, "Hi Suzie!" Again, she did not respond. She was looking right at my face, but seemed not to see me. As though I was no more than a glass window. Mocking eyes of other customers fixed on me, burning a hole into my neck. Got up. And without a word, marched out.

I started walking. Making sure to stay away from where last night's pummeling of the girl in white jeans incident occurred. THAT'S WHAT I GET FOR TRYING! It was another unseasonably mild night.

I don't get it. I don't get it, at all. I could understand—if she turned me down. But, why TOTALLY ignore me? Either I'm crazy or she's crazy. Or, we're both crazy. The hell with the Rainbow. From now on, I eat at home and save money.

I vow to forget tonight. I need to be more calculating and self-centered. Yes, that's the way it must be. The energy of the anger has cleared up my head. I feel more alive. I need to hold on to that.

I passed four check-cashing centers, a Gothic cathedral, and three Blockbuster video superstores.

On air, I walked, tirelessly.

Cut through half-a-dozen schoolyards, across one highway and over another.

Stopped to talk to a homeless man, on a dead-end, dog-litter minefield of a street. And turned, to walk away—when they appeared and blocked my path. They let him run away.

Their leader was a tall, well-built, light-skinned black man, with a shaved head. He wore a full-length black leather coat and stood directly in front of me, about five feet away. Silently, arms crossed. Eyes on me.

He was flanked on each side by a bull-headed, stocky, white midget in a tank-top. The pair cast their flat stares on my kneecaps. Each midget focusing on the kneecap closest in line to his position.

I knew I had to act quickly, because, any moment, the leader would signal for the gang to attack. My plan—blitz the leader. Thereby, scaring off the two sawed-off minotaurs, and making it one on one.

Not many guys in this predicament could pull that off. And I was not one of them.

I readied myself for a runaway charge through the curbside midget into the night, when an eerie sense of clear headedness possessed me...And the fingers of my now raised hands danced a spell on the leader of the ominous threesome. His body dissipated. All that was left of him was his cleanly shaven head, which now rolled like a brown bowling ball, away, off the curb into the gutter.

If that spell worked so thoroughly to obliterate a menacing gang leader, imagine what it would do to you! The midgets did.

It was 9:00 PM when I returned home. A man in charge, I sat in my loveseat and promptly fell into a dreamless sleep.

I awoke almost two hours later, feeling like a wooden board. Needing to walk that off, I took a light jacket from the closet, and headed out.

A street cooling breeze massaged my being. I loosened. Turned up my jacket collar, and contemplated in which direction to walk. The block where the girl in white jeans was pummeled must be avoided. And the way to the Rainbow was now also out. South, was acceptable. Because I always preferred to be within striking distance of the Rainbow, I hadn't walked south in quite a while. Maybe there'd be a new diner. I'd have coffee. There was a bounce to my steps. Yes, I thought, the resourceful heroism that I exhibited against the gang earlier tonight was indeed closest to who I really am.

At the end of the block, I consider stopping, to mambo with a time-expired, shoulder-high parking meter, but for that I feel too self-conscious. Anyhow, I don't know how to mambo. I cross the street.

Under the lurid light of a lamppost, straight ahead about a quarter of a block—arms flail. LEG AFIRE! A lone woman beats her purse wildly against her thigh!

Unhesitatingly, I dash over to aid her, and see, not a fire raging on her leg, but a large red mutt of a dog fastened to her leg blindly humping!

"GET THAT FUCKING THING OFF ME!" She yells at me, from behind the swarming, light-brown curtain of her long, flying hair as she continues to beat the—evidently—sexually aroused dog on his big head with her purse. Which worked him up, even more.

But the son of a bitch didn't know what hit him after I unleashed a vicious running kick into his ribs—he crumbled. There was no fight in him.

A hero, I turned to the ruffled woman I had rescued, who now tossed her hair from her face—

"Suzie…! That waitress last night only looked like—"

"YOU! YOU FUCKING CREEP!" she shrieked, trembling finger damning my face. "YOU PROBABLY SET THIS WHOLE THING UP!"

Run

NYQ Books, 2016

Dominion

I live in the basement
but—like you—have rights
to the sky, so I hang El Greco's
"Toledo" on the wall facing
my easy chair. Swirling
blue-gray clouds, dark
ominous sky. Man's fate
hanging by a thread. Flood.
Okay. As long as it's not
only me. But the sky changes.
Alongside "Toledo," I hang
Magritte's "The Dominion
of Light." Nicely aligned puffy
white clouds soften a bright
blue sky. The paintings remained
until I, like George Jefferson,
moved on up. Atop a steep
as-a-wall NJ cliff high up

on floor 33. Here in the sky,
on a bright-blue day, I see
the unglamorous northern
Manhattan skyline across
the vast Hudson River,
and beyond, the enormous
blimp looms dumbly over
Yankee Stadium. Deeper into
the Bronx, 13-year-old me
sits at one end of our old
living-room sofa and my father
at the other. He's watching
another war documentary on TV.
I eye the heavy metal base table
lamp. The one I'll use to bash
in the back of his head, next time
he raises a hand against my mother.
If ever I'd had the chance.

Poe Park

It had nothing to do with kicks.

Just the need to slow the invasive
train of repetitious thoughts rolling
unrelentingly through my head.

Outside of Poe Park I'd usually
be able to cop downers.
This hot night was no exception.
Done deal.

Stepped into the empty park to swallow
the promise of stupor.

Block-long, it was mostly concrete
and broken glass. It was 1976, and
I couldn't care less that within a mile,
landlords were torching buildings
into cash and the Yanks were making
a pennant run.

Cut across the park...

At the far end, sitting on the stoop of an
old white-frame cottage, was a tattered
lone soul playing guitar and singing. Long
limp blond hair hid much of his face, as he
sang Simon & Garfunkel's *El Condor Pasa*.
"I'd rather be a hammer than a nail..."

I hadn't seen him in ten years (when we
sat shoulder to shoulder in 7th grade), but
here was my former classmate—Ivar Kertes—
singing to a squirrel. Ivar, who could swing
on clarinet and run like a Cadillac.

In class, to get my attention he'd gently
elbow me. "Look intelligent Theodore,"
he'd say, straight-faced, as he fingered
imaginary scraggle on his chin, to affect
serious contemplation.

No longer Ted, but Theodore, I'd follow.
Then we'd face the teacher.

Rivet our eyes on him as though our very
lives depended on it and scratch our hairless
twelve-year-old chinny-chin-chins. Every
day for one or two minutes straight, we
looked intelligent.

I heard Ivar had gone schizo.

The downs melted my mind slow. Running
into Ivar, I momentarily forgot how scared
I was—not of Ivar, but of my own mind.

Waited for him to break before warmly saying,
"Hey!"

He did a protrude-lower-lip-out-and-blow-air-up
move, blowing his hair from his face. Armageddon-
eyed, he smiled recognition.

Slurring, I asked, "Is it true your old man
was a Ukrainian Nazi collaborator and trained
your mutt to salute when he said *sieg heil?*"

"To hell with him!" said Ivar. "He's dead."

After assuring him that I'd buy another bottle,
I reached over and threw back a heartening hit
of his Wild Irish Rose. He plunged back into

"I'd rather be a hammer than a nail / Yes I would /
If I cou—ou—ould / I surely wou—"

"Ivar man!" I interrupted. "That hammer and nail
shit sucks."

Resting the guitar at his side, he raised the Wild
Irish to his lips and drained a long red swig.
Tossed the bottle *splattercrash* onto concrete.

"Theodore," he said, "it's the melody I love."

"I do too. It's an old Peruvian folk tune.
Simon stuffed it with hammers and nails."

Ivar rose to his feet.

As though he were unveiling the Temple of
Artemis, with a sweeping gesture of his right
arm he presented the old white-frame cottage.
Awestruck, he held the pose for a moment.

I beheld the cottage. Flaked clapboard paint
and broken multi-pane windows. Heavy chains,
secured by 2 padlocks, festooned the 2 front doors.

"Do you know who lived here, Theodore?"

"Yeah. The poet Poe."

"Yeah," he affirmed. "The poet Poe. The Bronx
was country then. And this was a fine little farm-
house. Poe rented it. Lived here with his wife. She
died young. Here, of TB. He lives on. I AM HE!"
As the sun set, he launched into *The Raven*.

Out on my feet, I fell to my knees.

Polio

Popeye had his spinach. Reagan had his jelly beans. Elvis had his curled lip.
Popeye was strong to the finish. Sinatra had his rat-pack. The Situation's
got his six-pack. The Kennedys had Marilyn. Travis Bickle had his mohawk.
W had his Godless smirk. One poet invokes Miles Davis in an attempt to
cop some cool. The emperor's got no clothes. Mojo died with Muddy
Waters. Supercalifragilisticexpialidocious. Bukowski had his wine & his
muse. Ali had the heart of a lion. The Clash had "White Riot." Shrewdest
guy I ever met often played the fool. Leadbelly had Stagger Lee. Lenny
Bruce had his smack & shtick. *Kill or be killed.* Jonas Salk invented the cure
and refused to accept a cent.

Tractus

for William Packard

The nightly ritual (washing down valium with
Heineken), while intently watching The Arsenio
Hall Show (muted) no longer knocked me out.
Turned to the wall for what crawled out my soul…

Knew I'd rather be dead,
than spend another day at the job.

Stopped showing up.

Took up poetry.

The teacher was a young woman. Everyone
seemed to know one another. They went around
the room for some kind of feelings check. No
talk of poetry. Broke into a cold sweat. Group
therapy? My turn, I passed. Finished the fight
I had with a guy coming in on the subway
when the teacher announced the end of class and
the one book required. Said it was by a colleague.
The title included the word *tractus*. On my way
out, I asked, "Will we be learning poetic devices?"
She replied, "You can do that on your own."
"Is that how you learned?" I asked. And didn't
wait for an answer.

I rode the unbridled guitar bursts of grunge king
Neil Young and wrote lyrics that sang. Another,
a la Randy Newman, jabbing needles into that what
needs needling. Cut costs like the dry cleaners and
cable. Dropped insurance. Read Coleridge and Buk.
Got a part-time job doing quality control at a Pez
factory. And wrote a song like no one but me.

Tried again.

In this man, even a half-wit could tell they sat
before a monumental teacher. Not because he had
the imposing stature of one who way back might've
played fullback or because of his gray beard
and great head of dark unkempt hair, but because
of his glaring vast knowledge and roaring laughter
of wakefulness. There was a cop, a supermodel,
and an astrophysicist in the class. A woman seated
up front peppered him with *daddy, daddy please notice
me* questions. He threw her out. It warmed my heart.
Here was my chance to get something right.

Reunion

You cried in class, when
President Kennedy was shot.
A cute girl, with red curls,
in a third-grade class filled
with smart kids whose moms
and dads made their dioramas.

I was put into that class, made
friends, felt nothing when
Kennedy was killed. You had
a crush on me. I was elected
class president. Maybe someday
you'd be my girlfriend.

So when I looked to see who,
in the car stopped for a red light,
was calling me, as I hung out
killing time on the Lydig Ave.
street corner of the Bronx
neighborhood that I'd never left,
I knew it was you. Even though
fifteen years had been snuffed.
"Hi Leslie," I said. "Ted, Ted-dy!"
she yelled, "I'm very late—phone-
book—Queens—Leslie Herman—
Herman—Herman! Phone me!"
And drove away.

At her apartment in Queens, she
said she'd gone to the state university
in New Paltz and left to hook-up
with the Moonies. That currently
she was temping. She got naked
and blasted a fart. Said she wanted
to suck my toes and looked to me
for her cue to start.

While I thought: my feet are
unwashed, I need more Tuinals,
did I run over that cop's foot
at the Whitestone Bridge tollbooth
after his open palm slammed
the hood of my borrowed car
and he ordered me to stop? Lighted
a Marlboro. Got up to leave. I can
only do it with whores.

The Turks

"Yes," said the driver of the nameless New Jersey bus.
"The last stop's 42nd and 8th in New York. Three dollars. Pay
when you get off." I stuffed my cash back into my pant pocket,
and considered taking the seat that was broken into chaise
lounge position of the converted school bus, before taking
a right-window seat in the middle. A lifetime of New York City
subway riding inured me from the remnant stench of unwashed
ass. The only other passenger was a well-groomed older man
seated on the other side on the aisle a couple rows in back
of me. To assure passengers that the dusky black-bearded
driver wasn't a terrorist, an American flag was affixed above
a stuffed Mickey Mouse seated on the driver's rear view mirror.
Mickey's legs blocked the mirror almost entirely. I slept...

until I was awoken by a booming two-way between the well-
groomed older man and a nondescript middle-aged man sitting
directly in front of me. They were speaking a foreign language.
I'd become immune to such rude loud conversations if I
could identify the language, but I couldn't recognize theirs.
And was about to tell the guy in front of me that I'd strongly
prefer not to hear them, but what calmly came out of my mouth
was, "What language are you speaking?" "Turkish," he replied.
"Oh," I said, "like the Ottoman Empire or immortal poet Nazim
Hikmet." In broken English, he sang the praises of his homeland.
Because I've spent well over 90% of my life pretending to listen
to what others are saying, I feigned listening while I drifted into
thinking of a girl who years back worked at Tower Records.

Her name was Fem and she too was Turkish. She was a painter
who worked in their classical music section. She said she only
liked music and art of the Baroque period, and was supposed
to have been born then. I wasn't sure when the Baroque period
was but liked what she said because modern times surely wasn't
working for me. Fem was a high-cheekboned snowflake, with dark
almond-eyes and flowing hair. An angel or a witch. When the bus
arrived at 42nd and 8th, I waited for the others to get off before
getting up and handing 3 bucks to the driver. He shook his head no,
gestured toward the street at the talkative Turk who just got off,
and said he'd paid my fare. As for Fem I'd asked her if she'd like to
go to the Metropolitan Museum with me. "I might," she said, smiling.

Quietism

No choice. Vocal cord paralyzed.
Only an exhausting stream of
a ghastly whisper. Something
from someone already dead. "I'm
a sick man! Please…" I'd wheeze
into the phone when working
the HMO. Otherwise, mouth shut.

Like when the feeder of pigeons,
my spacey longtime neighbor, Isis,
recoiled and said, "You look like hell!"
when we crossed paths in the hallway
upon my release from the hospital.
If I had my voice I would've said,
"May the dirty pigeons turn on
you and slowly peck you to death."

Stayed home. Reflecting. Consoled
myself that I'd rather be voiceless
than sightless. Then tried to trick God
into resurrecting my voice by praying
for the callous Isis. And swore I'd
remain a man of few words, except
for poetry readings.

On my way home from another useless
visit to the kindly speech therapist,
I decided to stand in the long line
for a Domino's Pizza grand-opening
giveaway. Two slices left when
the server hands the woman ahead
of me a slice. She hands it back, saying
she wants the other one. The bigger
one. Leaving me…Ordinarily, I
would've said something. Anything.

Home again. Reflecting. Beyond my-
self. Realized that the vanity plate
wasn't the most American of all things.

Had to be the laugh track or the idling
engine…The angelic drummer-girl
Karen Carpenter's singing was worthy
of Homer's Sirens…. And the spirits
of the dead don't ride the wind. A year
passed. And then my voice returned.
Was it God's will? I was deeply grateful….
And then took it for granted.

No Evidence of a Tumor

"You got a nice dick," she says. Toy voice like a flute. The appraiser.
Strokes it. Planet Ass in my face. HOT DIGGITY DOG ZIGGITY
BOOM! But what's this *nice* shit? The way she says it, I know she
means *nice* like you say after watching your team turn an around
the horn double play. Or how I felt when I saw my next door neighbor's
cockatoo fly out the window. She's a blunt, tough little nut, but I've
got to…"Big enough?" "Just right," she says. And she knows dicks.
Really. Night of many not so slight exquisite deaths. *Just right.* Two
syllables. Delivered just right. Syllable for syllable, beating the eight
uttered by the doctor years later after yet another surgery.

Decoder Poem

When they say,
I feel your pain.
They really mean—
Even your pain
is theirs to claim.

When they say,
*Some things you
shouldn't
have to pay for.*
They really mean—
They're scheming
24/7
to make you pay.

When they say,
*There are two sides
to every story.*
They really mean—
Whatever side you're on
they'll take the other.

When they say,
I've made peace with it.
They really mean—
They'll take it to the grave.

When they say,
Buy one get one free.
They really mean—
They've quadrupled
the price of one.

When they say,
their parents did
the best they could.

They really mean—
They would've
been better off
being brought up
in an orphanage.

When they say,
Fifty is the new forty.
They really mean—
They're pushing sixty.

When they say,
So sorry to hear that.
They really mean—
Your sorrow is
their sustenance.

When they say,
He's like family.
They really mean—
They're paying him less
than the minimum wage.

When they say,
Don't be a stranger.
They really mean—
They rue the day
you were born.

When they say,
No cause for alarm.
Consider suicide.

Grand Prix

The '71 2-door baby-blue
black hardtop Pontiac Grand
Prix was 10 years old, but had
low mileage and was mint
when I bought it for $1,000
from an old woman up in
Tarrytown, who only drove
it twice a week to and from
the A&P. Otherwise, she kept
the 400-horsepower Coke-bottle-
shaped muscle car with automatic
everything in her garage. I never
asked why she ever owned
such a car. I did know that I'd
struck gold. An enterprising guy
could easily double his money.
I wasn't enterprising. Nor was
I a car guy, and this was very
much a car guy car. But in my gut,
I knew it had to be mine.

Parked by the P.S. 105 Bronx
schoolyard, the very next day
I sat behind the wheel, next to
a drug dealer named—believe-it-
or-not—Paul Bunyan, who I got
on with okay but was a prick
and bully. On and on he went
about how much he loved
the Grand Prix. When a kid
on the street stared at the car
and us, Bunyan savored saying,
"What're you lookin' at, sonny?"
I revved the engine, which roared
a testicle-quaking riot. He got out
and looked back, unleashing
a shit-eating grin.

Blacked-out at a Long Island
disco. Myles took over the wheel
going home. By this time
the Grand Prix was plenty
dented from months of me
driving stoned: through
a garage door, into a subway
pillar, etc. Myles had mainlined
a speedball, had a glass eye,
no license, and used his left
foot for the brake, his right
for the gas pedal, and was coolly
resigned to an early death.
We couldn't find our way out
of an area where palatial homes
mocked us. From the back,
Myles' younger brother, Jay, said,
"Let's pull a Charles Manson."

Stoned, I drove to a singles
mixer in Manhattan. Hit it off
with a nurse named Ahuva.
Like the vacuum cleaner, she
said. Vacuum cleaner, indeed.
She was a ripe white pear,
and had a nice place on the Upper
East Side. Next morning I gave
the doorman a that's-right-I'm-
fucking-her-and-it's-not-costing-
me-a-penny-and-thanks-for-
holding-the-door-for-me-smiley,
good-bye.

But forgot where I parked.
Couldn't find the car. Clueless.

Hours later, the same forces
that protected while in the Grand
Prix delivered. At a red light,
a guy pulled up alongside of me.
Asked how much I wanted for it.
I said, $1,000. And that was that.
Or so I thought.

Because many nights, many years,
I'd dream, searching for my Grand Prix.
No longer though, I hate to say.

My Sister Tells Me

for Dr. Barbara R. Greenberg

After she told mom
old Ben of Ben's Hobby Shop
urged her and other little
girls to climb the ladder
and look at items shelved
highest so he could look
up their skirts, mom
marched in with her.

After she got caught
shoplifting Turkish Taffy
from Bib & Sam's street
corner candy store, mom
took her to Woolworth's
on White Plains Road,
bought her marbleized
pencils, so that she'd no
longer feel deprived.

After she told mom
2 girls at school snatched
her wooly white pom-pom
hat during recess and flung
it to and fro playing saloogie
mom told her what to say
to the bigger one. She did.
It didn't happen again.

She didn't have to tell me
how proud mom was when,
at age 9, she won the school
spelling bee. Or how proud
mom would've been had she
survived beyond her beloved
Basia Roza's tenth birthday,
to see her lop heads from
the hydra we call life.

The Paisley Shirt

I liked going to Fordham Road with my mom.
We'd take the 12A bus to the block-after-block
hustle-bustle Bronx shopping stretch. When I
was ten, my mother took me there, to Alexander's
department store, to buy me a couple of shirts
for the coming school year. The store was grand,
it had everything. But what I liked most of all
was being there with her. She was kind, pretty,
and young. She bought what we could afford, 2
bargain bin paisley shirts. Afterwards, we walked
a few blocks to the RKO Fordham to see "The Sound
of Music." But I can't say I liked the homely Miss
Hathaway of "The Beverly Hillbillies" look-alike
belting out how the "hills come alive."

When I wore one of the shirts to school, the jaunty
male teacher announced to the entire class that
another kid, Lucas Ortiz, and I were wearing identical
shirts, like he was shocked that 2 boys in the same
crowded working-class 4th grade Bronx classroom
would be sporting the same cheap shirt. The paisley
shirt my mother chose. Shielded by the fashion
faux pas, he pleasured in shaming us. My face flushed
red heat. Shame trumped rage but I blurted, fuck you.
And Lucas, who perhaps didn't even care about
the teacher's crack, had to outdo me, hurling a chair.
But I didn't blurt fuck you, and Lucas didn't hurl
a chair. Shame stuck to my gut, the shirt, to my back.

Elementary School

Squat & curl up
under desk should
the commies come
dropping bombs.

Men with cool
names like Vasco
De Gama were first
to sail straight to
India, and Ponce
De Leon, looking
for the fountain
of youth, was first
to set foot in Florida.

Johnny B. would
show off chomping
down chalk, Louis
could be tricked
into drinking piss.

We could watch
my Jew, Jack Ruby
shoot to death
the 3 named goon
who shot to death
our golden President
on live television

Boys in size-place
order, meant me
wanting to be taller.

When the father
of our country was
a boy he couldn't tell
a lie, and confessed
to chopping down
a cherry tree.

We warred against
the people of North
Vietnam on account
of a Domino Theory.

Mondays meant
white shirts & green
ties to assembly,
all of us singing
of stout hearted
men, who'd stand
shoulder to shoulder
& fight to the end...

It was cooler to like
The Byrds, dumb
"Mr. Tambourine Man,"
than Barbara Mason's
heady & soulful
"Yes, I'm Ready."

Plotnik could be hung
by his collar on a hook
and left there all day
in a closed closet.

Everyone had a right
to their own opinion.
And everyone had one.

Kill (2)

The music video. I don't care
who directs it. Although I know
it's not Kubrick.

The hoarder who lives below me,
before he kills me with his stench
arsenal of mothballs and decay.

Those who'd privatize social security.
Their families. Harvest all organs.
Piss on their bones.

That fat-ass plaque in Yankee Stadium's
monument park, dedicated to the team's
late swinish owner, Steinbrenner.

Those who try to sell us Mariah Carey
and Maggie Gyllenhaal as foxes. Or as
you might say, "hotties." But I won't.

Corporate interests & pedophiles.
Former first. If it's good for them—
it's bad for you. Real bad.

Any past or present reference
to Madonna as a diva.

The price-gouge cost
of generic stool softener
at the Good Neighbor Pharmacy
in Guttenberg, New Jersey.

The willfully ignorant.

The Rock and Roll Hall of Fame.
Turn it into a bingo parlor, a whore-
house, or a lottery superstore.

Any poet who, when giving a reading,
asks if he has time for one more.
Less is more. More or less.

Anyone who doesn't inherently
get the difference between
earning money and *making* it.

Anyone with perfect bleached white teeth
and tattoos. Unless they sport a facial tattoo.

Socialized medicine for elected officials.

Bagism.
Tagism.
Ragism.
Tribalism.

The clueless who say, *What doesn't
kill you makes you stronger.*

Your right to use plastic
to buy a frappuccino.

Those who know me
but don't buy my books.

Vanity plates.
Except for:
NO CA CA,
Kvech22 &
IB6UB9.

Paul Janko

Snatched me
a yelping
white
toy-poodle.

He's John
the Revelator
incarnate, but
I call him
Nancy.

Now
we're three:
Nancy, me, and
357
Magnum (worth
every last cent).

So I can splatter
my pained brain
onto the ceiling
if need be.

And blow the
balls off he who
needs to have his
balls blown off.

On the mattress,
357
Magnum, Nancy
& me, watch our
favorite movie:
The Searchers.

John Wayne
doesn't
pretend
his kidnapped
pre-teen niece,
squaw of Comanche
Chief Scar,
is redeemable.

Like me,
he knows
what has been
fucked
cannot be
un-fucked.

The Suspect

Alone in the backseat of the unmarked
cop car, I was still in a state of shock,
when Detective Blarney Stone, who
was riding shotgun, turned and said
something to me; so I couldn't really
hear what it was he said, but could see
that the threads of his bulbous nose
were more purple than red.

Because I had yet to reply, he
again asked, "Do you like to fuck
your girlfriend in the ass?"

I'd been driving to the laundromat
that night, 2 full sacks at my side,
when I found myself surrounded
by wailing sirens and cop cars.
Then I was whisked into one while
my own car was cop-commandeered,
a big scene in my neighborhood. Did
I run a light? No. Hit and run? No.
Had I vowed *never* to be taken alive?

And what of this asshole's
asshole inquiry? I answered
honestly, "I don't have
a girlfriend."

Well-tailored walrus, Detective
Armani Meatball, slammed
the brakes, hard eyed me and said,
"You don't have a girlfriend?"
The 2 masters of my fate gazed
lovingly at one another, as if to say,
He's our man, let the fun begin.

At the eerily unoccupied police
station, they said I could leave
anytime, but we needed to talk

about the mangled dead body
of a girl found on the rooftop of
one of the many 5 story walk-ups
on my block: Front-page killing
that I'd heard and read about.

Was I truly free to leave? Yes.
Why didn't I? From the get-go
they pressed me to let them
into my place, where I'd punched
holes into a door, covered a wall
with news clippings about "Jaws,"
and had drugs. I figured a bleary-
eyed judge might grant a search
warrant. I needed them off me.

Was there a shred of evidence
linking me? No. Did I know
where I was on the night of...?
No. Did I agree to take a ride
downtown for a lie detector
test? Yes. Did I pass the test?
Yes. Did I agree to bite into
wax? Yes. Bite marks match
the killer's? No. Was I questioned
further and kept waiting there
in limbo all night, anyway?
Yes. Was the slightly torn back
seat of my car ripped open,
and the glove compartment
broken into. Yes. The misshapen
sacks meant they'd also rifled
through the dirty laundry,
but that they put back.
Three short lines a year later,
in the Police Blotter section,
of the *New York Daily News,*
the case had been cracked.

The adult son of the old lady
who lived next door to the girl.
The other side of the wall,
to be exact. He didn't live
there, but visited often.

Why me? I'd often have coffee
at the Kingsbridge Diner,
at times drugged-up nodding
into last night's box scores. Deb,
a waitress there, was friendly
with cops who'd stop in. One
must've told her the girl's nose
had been bitten off, because Deb
liked sharing that unreported
horror tidbit. She told me, and I
told her that I knew the victim
from the photo, vaguely recalling
her from back in high school.
Chatty Deb, had shot a bored
finger straight at me.

But fuck me—my car and laundry.
You might need not to believe it,
but what was plain in the air
was that these 2 enforcers of law
couldn't care less. Guilty or innocent,
their only aim, snatching a suspect,
making it stick, rising in rank
and sleeping like babies.

Jack Maurer a/k/a Trigger

You could stroll into the room
anytime Trigger was butt-naked,
getting it on with some stoned
skank. He'd pause and wave his big
hard on. Yet he couldn't piss into
a urinal if anyone was around,
and had to use a stall.

I Should've Helped Him Plot His Escape

Our third floor window faced
the back of another six-story
apartment building. Between
the buildings was a concrete alley.
The building was close enough
so that I could've hit it under-
handed with a Spaldeen. Its sole
balcony was on the second floor.
And although the railed balcony
was as long as that entire side
of the building only one apartment
had access. Through an unpainted
wooden door. The door the woman
would shove the boy out of.

She'd wear a floral apron over her
housecoat and her gray hair tied
tightly in a bun. The boy was about
my age, eight. She looked too old
to be his mother. An otherwise
ordinary looking boy, he was always
dressed up. Slacks, shoes shined,
and a button up short sleeved shirt
in warm weather. A well-scrubbed
little man. Too well scrubbed. I never
saw him on the street. And I never
saw him at school. She'd shove him
out the door, and he'd beg to play
with other kids. Every day, he'd
be left on the balcony—

Alone. No ball. No books. Nothing.
Looking up, down, every which way,
arms at times windmills, he'd pace
and skip for hours. Stopping only
when she'd come out. Stone-faced,
she'd hand him a bowl of mush
and a spoon. But there was nothing
to rest it on. He'd eat standing.

I slid the window open, "Hey!"
I called out to him. He stopped
skipping and looked up at me.
"I'm Ted," I said, and asked
what his name was. "David!"
he shouted excitedly. I invited
him to come out and play. She
must've heard talk and came
bustling out. But when David
pointed to our window and said,
"Look mommy, I made a friend
up there!"—I ducked—and she
dragged him in, screeching
"Mommy will be upset if you
get kidnapped! Mommy will
be upset if you get kidnapped…!"

Getting Some

Thirteen, hair & drawl
like Elvis, his own
back-boned swagger,
he moves to my block
from some distant state.
Within 6 months he makes
out with half the girls in
the neighborhood. Some
a year older than us.
He's asked to play bass
in a local rock band.
Doesn't even plug in.
Why his family moved to—
of all places—the Bronx?
Might have to do with why
he's placed straight into
our grade's class for psychos.
Having never really made
out with a girl on my own,
I'm drawn to the guy. He joins
our crowd. I call for him.

His 12-year-old sister lets
me in. She looks like him,
and although it somehow
comes together better on
her brother, there's nothing
I don't like about her. Kisses
my mouth. Shocks me.
Waves me on to follow—
into her room. *His* sister.
You don't go for a friend's
sister. I stay put in the hall.
He steps out of her room
carrying a girl bride-style.
Both rumpled, but clothed.

Her ass is a nectarine. "She's
a whore," he says. Nods
at me, "Come get some."
"I'm a whore," says the girl,
boldly. His sister yells,
"If my brother & his friend
wanna rape you let 'em."

High Noon at Midnight:
Loomis vs. Mr. Havoc

Laughing his ass off, he spat
on a stylish man walking
a small dog. Then he spat on
the dog. They fled. Raining
close range coughs onto
the back of her head, he
chased a trim gym-bag toting
woman, as she too fled. Havoc
kicked over a street-corner
trash can now, looked into
the 99th Street night and eye-
balled a gangly, bespectacled,
bald guy across the street.

This was Loomis. His arm
around a parking meter as he
nursed a container of coffee.
This decent but tightly-wound
sleepless loner. Juvenile Diabetes.
Thirty-eight. Failing eyesight,
numb feet. Rage! He wanted
a wife & children. Unmoved,
watching the goon carry on,
he readied for violence. High
noon at midnight, Havoc
stomping his way.

Loomis spilled the remaining
coffee onto the street, placed
the container down at the foot
of the parking meter, took 2
steps back onto the middle of
the sidewalk, crossed his arms,
and set his blurry sights on
the oncoming threat. As he took
step one onto the curb, Loomis,
flashing stiff forefingers at him
shouted, "Hey!"

Havoc stopped, eyed Loomis.
Loomis then used his foot to
ghost a line on the sidewalk in
front of where he stood. "Cross
that line...I'm taking an eye!"
Took a step back. Placed his
hands behind him. Up to the line
Havoc stepped—

Stopped.

Eye to eye, an arm's length
apart. Loomis white. Havoc
black. Both were lanky,
and about the same height.
Unlike the much larger black
man who turned the corner—
walking straight into this.

"What's the problem, brother?"
he said to Havoc, handing
him a buck, before adding,
"You best get going."

Trying to downplay the fact
that Loomis had scared him
stiff, Havoc laughed a phony
face-saving laugh, and walked.
His patron moved on.

Loomis was alone.

From a window:
"He's homeless! Crazy!"

"Not crazy enough!" said Loomis.

Old news to me.

Protection

Why would some little kid
spit into my little kid face
for no reason with my father
standing nearby? Not because
he expected to get his head
slammed by an open adult
hand. That same hand then
slammed me. My father not
saying a word to the kid or
me before, during or after.

Later that day the kid's father
called out to us on the street.
He was bigger than my father,
yet he kept his distance and said
something about "Next time you
hit my kid…" Exuding a bring it
on calm, my father said nothing.
I'd never seen him that calm,
surely not when he was beating
my mom or boasting about real
& imagined violence. His calm
unsettled me. Even when he was
seated alone lost in television
his unhinged rage-filled energy
caused my gut to tighten.

I'm unsure if it was before or after
the time my father asked me to step
out of our apartment into the hall
with him to show off his gun by
blasting what he said were blanks
at a wall, but I do know a year
or two had passed since the little
kid spitting episode, because now
around age ten and out on the street
alone, I was in a shoving match

with another kid over who knows what,
when both the kid and his father started
chasing after me. Figuring this grown
man's gonna kick my ass I took off
escaping across an empty lot.

I didn't tell my father about it,
never told him anything about
anything, knew to keep his nasty
scrambled head out of things.
I was protecting him,
my sole inescapable enemy.

Falling

Seated beside me in the front row of the theater's
balcony, my friend said he was frightened by the over-
whelming urge to hurl himself over the low railing.
No joke. He was mired in dread. His eyes though were
not resigned to death. Unclenching my teeth, I let him
know that I'd already imagined myself locked in
a life-or-death clinch with the harmless stranger seated
at my side, and was now frightened that when I stand
a demon in the row behind will calmly shove me.

Where I'm Coming From

Happy to board the retired school bus
turned dollar van just before the driver
said, "No more," I'd have taken any seat
for the hour or so trip. But there were none
left so I resigned myself to getting off,
when the driver got up and led me to
the back where there was a folding chair
that I hadn't seen in the aisle. I wouldn't
have to wait for the next bus. "Oh, I didn't
notice the executive seat," I quipped.
"NOW YOU DID!" shouts a guy seated
in front of me to my left without looking
at me. Damn, I said to myself, that's shut-
the-fuck-up funny shit he unloaded on me.
He rested a heavy hand on his leg. The
leg was spread well into the aisle. It was
the reason why I didn't spot the folding
chair when I first got on.

The scale in my head then tipped from
the funny to the shut-the-fuck-up. He had
taunted me. Like I was some kind of Mr.
Fancy pants. That what I'd said implied
that I was too good for the folding chair.
I'm too good for that entire bus.
But that's not where I was coming from. I
tapped an idiot kid seated next to me on
the shoulder. He took off his headphones
and turned to me. His mouth scowled
but his eyes said curious. Smiling, I said,
"You know I'm sitting in the moneymaking
seat." A stony long moment passed,
then he brightened and said, "Oh, you
mean like it don't really belong here?"
"Yeah," I said, aiming my words at
the back right of my enemy's fat head,
"I don't begrudge these drivers doing
whatever they need to make an extra buck."
But gone were the days I would've added,
"And if not for someone's leg…"

The Gambler

I was playing after school
head-on $1/$2 poker against
my friend Gene's fat gout-
afflicted mother at their place
when the doorbell rang.
"No one else here," I said.
"You want me to get that?"

"Get what?!" she said.

At the door was a handsome
black woman in an ivory,
medium brim church hat.
"My son's in jail," she said.
"But he didn't do anything
I can't forgive him for."

"Can I sleep in his bed?" I asked.

"Yes," she said, fading away.
I shut the door. Got back to
the game, and sat. Gene's
mother was shuffling the deck.

"My mind's not mine," I said.

"Yeah, well I didn't hear no
doorbell," she said. "Anyhow,
you're the same sandbagging
faggot to me. Splash cold water
in your eyes."

"No," I said. "We're about even.
One cut. High card takes all."

"Sure," she said.

And drew a deuce…

I drew the Jack of Hearts.

"HA!" barked Gene, lunging
for the cash. Unnoticed, he'd let
himself in. "You 2 degenerates
are into me for plenty," he said
pocketing what he snatched.

Vesti la Giubba

While I wondered who was more irresistible to women,
Tiger Woods or Pablo Picasso, everyone in the subway car
was suddenly roused by a woman announcing, "I am a
struggling opera singer." That she didn't lead with *sorry
for the interruption* was a plus. I looked up and saw it
wasn't a woman, but a filthy little wisp of a white guy,
his lightly hooded head bowed. "I will sing *"Vesti la giubba"*
from *Pagliacci*," he said. I closed my eyes and allowed myself
to be moved by his subdued and heartfelt tenor. The other
riders were mostly well-dressed young college grads who
flocked to the island of Manhattan, and work very, very
long hours, looking to make their mark and/or to find a mate.
This opera-singing beggar, I knew, didn't have the singing or
begging chops to separate any of these go-getters from a thin
dime. I would seize the compassion-flaunting moment. They
needed to be shown that they were "less than." Led by his
enduringly bowed, hooded head, the singer of opera shuffled
silently through the car. Head to toe, his clothes were once all
white. I reached over and showcased an Abe Lincoln into his open
palm. He didn't say thank you, which was also a plus. Nor did
he call on God to bless me. It wasn't like he had pull with God,
like Tiger Woods or Pablo Picasso.

The Man Who Conquered the World

He married, fathered a boy
& a girl, toiling 7 twelve-hour
days a week behind the wheel
of a NYC cab to make ends
meet. So it was no surprise
he looked tired in the photos
from twenty or so years ago
that his daughter shared at her
wedding party. Months before
the wedding date he'd been fine,
then one day the doctor said
he had lung cancer. His son
& daughter alternated taking
off a week at a time from their
professional lives to be stationed
at his hospital bedside. Sleepless
nights in the nearby recliner. He
died there, but had long since
been fulfilled by how his kids
turned out. This man who years
back had come to scorn his wife
because she ignored or berated
their kids but stayed married
solely to remain under the same
roof as them, caring for & enjoying
his kids, taking off every other
Sunday when they'd tickle
his feet before sunrise rousing
him from much needed sleep.
Happy, he'd get up, loving them
more than he cared for himself.

True Cool

After rolling a thunderous strike to open the game,

Brian Jones haircut-topped Stan Conley rolled 7

more straight to put the heavily betted match away.

Without a word, he then collected his part of the win-

nings from his backslapping backers, kicked off his

rented bowling shoes and slipped back into his black

ankle-length roach killer boots before walking off.

He didn't give a shit about the chance to bowl

a perfect game. Complete in bright red turtleneck he

looked British Invasion, but they said he was a junkie.

Thirteen, I knew that was fucked up, but so what.

Turtles

A kid standing several steps from the man-made lake
was readying to make the running jump onto the large
rock where turtles were lounging. This really bugged me
because it was a given that he was up to no good, and I
like turtles, the way they lazily hang out, don cool armor,
and mind their own fucking business. I was about to say
something to him, but he was with another fourteen or
fifteen year old, and they had a pit bull so I mutely walked
past, continuing my first lap on the paved path around
the lake, stopping a few times to look back, only to see
that the kid has gone from doing shoulder rolls to trunk twists
and back to shoulder rolls. He was posing. I might not have
had the balls to say anything, but he didn't have the balls
to chance that jump. His delay all but assured me that if he
were to give it a go now he'd likely come up soaked or hurt.
Hopefully, he'd crack his head bloody on a rock. His body
left afloat in the lake overnight, like that of a turtle I'd seen
the day before. A turtle that I'm sure didn't die a natural death.

I'd understand if there were girls around. He'd show the girls
how he could fly, show them a turtle up close, but there weren't
any girls around. More likely he was the kind who drowned
stray cats. I could also understand if there was a sheep
on the rock and he wanted to hump it, but it was a turtle.
I may be a straight male but that doesn't mean I'm inter-species
love phobic. Okay, so he's an every boy daredevil. I get it.
But really, like everything else, it all comes back to yours truly.
Teenage boys and pit bulls always bring me down. Turtles
lift my spirits. I kept walking. And distracted myself reading

214

official signs: Welcome to Hudson County Nature Trails at North Hudson Park, Keep off Lake Thin Ice, and Trout Stocked Water Woodcliff Lake (stapled to a tree), sidestepping people who simply because they could were using their cell phones to take pictures of one another. While slob fishermen sat on folding chairs, hands free, next to their multiple rod set ups.

Upon completing the first of my 3 or 4 almost mile-long laps around the lake, back to what I'll call turtle rock, I see the same fucking kid holding a turtle. "I see you worked up the nerve to make the jump," I say. "I hope you're gonna put that turtle back." "Yeah," he says. "I wouldn't do anything to hurt the turtle." Pleased with myself and feeling hopeful, I walked on. I unzipped my hip sack and took out my large padded headphones and tiny ipod, listening only through one ear to stave off the tinnitus that had begun in the other. My mood had cooled so I started with a mellow but soulful mix of artists like Glen Campbell, Dionne Warwick, and The Carpenters.... After Campbell's sweet and melancholy "Wichita Lineman," came Karen Carpenter's "Rainy Days and Mondays Always Bring Me Down," but like I said, teenage boys and pit bulls always bring *me* down, so I thumbed a Lester Young playlist on my ipod and lost myself in his melodic airborne sax. When I reached turtle rock after my third lap the kid, his friend, and dog were no longer there. A woman holding a little girl's hand stood by, telling her, "Because the turtle is upside down." So that's what that funky looking fleshy thing that I'd seen before was, a turtle on its back. The kid had flipped the turtle on its back. Funny thing though, I'd noticed that turtle on its back before he was on the scene, but had my distance Ray Bans on and the sky had turned gray, so I didn't know what I was looking at. It could've been anything from a human brain or intestines to a live giant vagina. But I knew that the kid had to have something to do with it.

With every step, I was getting more and more pissed. When I was his age I know I could've made that same running jump. But back then I didn't give a rat's ass about turtles. I needed to get into *the zone*. Like when I was the only kid who was able to throw the ball through the tire hole from shallow left field on day one of little league tryouts, or when I hand-snatched a horsefly mid-air. I knew I'd get both of those feats done right before I did them. I needed to access the zone to make the running jump, and set the turtle upright. Or fuck myself up trying…. Or maybe I could find a really long branch. Fuck the branch. Bent on making the jump I began the march back to Turtle Rock, but suddenly realized that you can't channel the zone, the zone channels you. So I did the next best thing, looping the Sturm und Drang of Black Sabbath's "War Pigs," to psych myself to fever pitch. I was a commando. Spotting the two boys and their dog in the not too far off park, I thought of calling out to them, telling the kid that maybe he could make the jump again and undo what *someone* did. But no, this was on me. War Pigs. Hello death.

When I got there the upside down turtle was gone! This was truly a miracle. I wouldn't have to give up my body. Vital, since I was now aware that even if I made the running jump onto the rock, I'd need to make the same jump back without a running start. A feat the kid couldn't do either. That's when I saw that there were 2 large rocks inches below the water line. The kid likely took off his sneakers, rolled up his pants, and stepped over to snag a turtle. I was right all along. The posing kid didn't have the balls. I could've done the same. Flummoxed, I wondered how an upside down turtle could get off a rock. It was by the edge of the rock. Had one or more of the other turtles nudged the upside-downer into the water? Hell no, that was wishful thinking. I needed to know. An elderly couple walked towards me, the woman clutching a pair of large brown stuffed animals against her chest. The husband seemed embarrassed. I made sure not to stare at them, needlessly fiddling with my headphones instead. A bunch of imbeciles passed before I stopped a power-walker, filled him in, and asked if he'd seen anything. "It's hard to believe," he said. "But what you saw was a turtle that has only the rim of its shell. He's very spunky and basks among the others on that rock most days." "Wow!" I say. How could the shell come off? Nodding towards the lake, he says, "Who knows what goes on down there? "Not me" I say. "But I sure as shit know what goes on up here."

House Call

Hadn't seen Duke in over
twenty years, but last night
we knew each other as soon
as our paths crossed in Penn
Station. So I got to ask him
about something I'd heard
way back. Had to do with his
beer truck driver father,
who named him for former
Brooklyn Dodger great Duke
Snider, and often stood on
the top stoop of their walk-up,
smoking a cigar, and keeping
an eye on kids playing street
games. Kids like runty Ira Fox
who lived in the flat below them,
and would stickball-bat-clang
the steam pipes to signal he
was coming up to visit. Was it
true that when young hot shot
heart surgeon Dr. Ira Fox showed
up in the old neighborhood
to visit his mother, your father
made him give him a check-up
on the top stoop? Duke said
yeah. Ira leapt 2 steps at a clip.
and nodded hello, looking to fly
by Duke & his father, but Duke's
father stepped in front of him
and raised his palm for Ira to stop,
and unbuttoning his Hawaiian
shirt so Ira could ear-to-chest
check his bare chest. He checked
his pulse, too. "Good!" said Ira.
"Foxy," said Duke, "don't forget
how my dad looked out for you
if he ever needs cuttin' up."

Mercy

"Meeting on the internet and the thousand-
plus miles distance between us added
to the allure. He was 28. I'm already 35.
The first weekend we met in the flesh
was nothing but bliss. But, I ended up
pregnant. No, neither of us planned on that.
Having endured a childhood spent shuffled
among foster homes, he wanted to make
it right. He proposed marriage. I happily
accepted. After all, don't I deserve a family
of my own? On day 2 of his 2 day drive
to the ceremony, the engine of his car
broke down. We rescheduled the marriage.
In the interim I miscarried. I was shattered.
He was a comfort, said, together, we'd see
it through. The next day, he calls the whole
thing off. My mom said to pretend the whole
thing never happened. The therapist said
there are no quick fixes. Really, I don't feel
like living anymore. I still can't believe it."
I assure her, "The baby was unborn to spare
you from a lifetime of marital misery." I don't
believe it, but no one can say for sure it's a lie.
And if it happened tomorrow, I'd say it again.

Thrilla in Manila

Whites had long since fled
the Bronx's Grand Concourse
leaving me, the sole guy at
the Loews Paradise theater
for the live, big screen showing
of the "Thrilla in Manila" who
wasn't Black or Puerto Rican.
And no, that didn't make me
uptight. Being expected to know
formal dining etiquette, that
would've made me uptight.

Among the first to gain entrance,
I took an aisle seat & a swig
from my fifth of Smirnoff vodka.
Someone tapped my shoulder,
a powerful looking guy behind
me wanting some. He was already
rocking & after throwing back
a prodigious swig of mine he laughed
& laughed, while repeating, "I'm
crippled for life." He was an ox,
but his self-assessment was fine
by me. Fixed on his mantra we
laughed on through round one.
Then he disappeared.

The crowd was roaring 50/50
Frazier/Ali. *You* thought they
would be wildly Ali? What do
you know? Me, I hoped the fight
would beat the hype, "Smokin'
Joe" & "The Greatest," delivering.
I wanted to witness history.

Every inch as valiant as Achilles,
Smokin' Joe Frazier sat on his stool
after his trainer threw in the towel.
The clash had been epic. I emptied
the bottle, someone passed me a joint,
the place stayed raucous, and if that ain't
inner-city you can kiss my ass.

The Rise & Fall of Billy Horst

When Teresa walked past the street
corner where we were hanging out
you shouted, "Slut!" and tossed
pennies at her feet. This confused me.
After all, you said that you *balled* her.
And although I'd never heard anyone
say balled before I knew it had to
be some kind of sex act conquest,
so why would you be mad at her?
But I dared not ask. A boy, I figured,
should be born knowing all that stuff.
And not only did you know stuff,
you had the baffling gift of gab,
shooting the shit with all walks of
life as though you shared a history.

No surprise you became a lawyer,
making tons of money, separating
insurance companies from some of
their loot. You could afford all vices
known to man times ten, and tuck wife
and kids away in a leafy cul-de-sac.

When Dix's car was wrecked, rear-
ended on the Cross Bronx, I advised
him to call you. Since he wasn't badly
injured, you took on the open-and-shut
case "only as a favor for an old friend."
Tapped out, Dix was keenly aware
that this business could go on forever.
Still, he was pleased.

I was in the lobby of a club in Yonkers,
where Felix Cavaliere was featured,
when I ran into her. "Teresa?" I asked.
She talks marriage, kids, divorce,
remarriage, and before I could utter
another word, says she was "a stick
with small tits," an only child of older

parents. Then, after you'd gained their
trust, you went and tore off her blouse,
tried to rape her. You stayed pissed
because she fought you off.

Forever came. You lost the case for Dix.
Zero. Shattered, he called me. I called
you, and was blown off, "I never liked
the guy," you said. "Anyway, he always
was full of shit." Dix had trusted you,
but when the shock of *zero* eased some,
Dix coldly reviewed the case, showing
many instances of gross mishandling to
me. He said you'd sold him out to get
a quick payout from the same insurance
company on a big money case. Having
steered him to his unmaking, I felt tainted.
But Dix never held it against me. He
married, moved out west, and turned
himself into a big success.

Try as he would Dix couldn't shake
the hatred he carried for you. Never
could forget how you buried him.
Figuring sleaze like you had to have
enemies, he hired a detective to look
into your ever-thriving practice.

For about the same amount you'd spend
on a high-end hooker, he was informed
you'd set up a hospital x-ray tech hot line.
Illegal, but you wanted an edge. A tech
who wasn't on your payroll felt left out.
And as Dix laughingly says, he "dropped
a dime." You fought the case and lost.
Didn't serve time but were disbarred.
Last I heard you were trying to make
a buck as a go-between, selling a painting.
Then you were dead.

No Reason Why

Looking down at the sickly orange liquid and jagged
shards of glass on the sidewalk, I damn well know
that if the bottle of orange soda tossed from a window
of a tall apartment building had landed a foot to the left
it would've exploded on top of my head. Sprawled in
a puddle of blood, I'd be too dead to be embarrassed
about being the sole winner of this lottery of the unlucky.
When a passerby calls the cops, I split,

and take shelter in the scrap paper chicken scratch
I pull from a back pocket: barber, bank, supermarket,
haircut, withdraw sixty bucks at Bank of America,
and buy a quarter pound of capicola ham, smoked turkey,
and a 3-pack of roach motels at Gristedes. Less than
an hour later, having completed all missions, I crumple
the list, and chuck it into a street corner garbage can.

Home, I place one trap below the kitchen sink, the other
2 on the bathroom floor, below the sink, and behind
the toilet. I'd rather swallow a roach than have one crawl
into my accessible asshole while I'm trying to take a shit.
Lunching on the smoked turkey, I ask myself who
it was who'd toss an unopened bottle of orange soda onto
a bustling street. I figure, a punk kid acting on a whim.
Although, for all I know it might've dropped out of the sky.

I then retrace my steps leading to my brush with death.
Did anything happen to throw off the timing of my move-
ments, thusly saving me from death? Someone on the street
bump me breaking my stride? Did a stranger stop me to ask
for the time? Was this an instance when the spirit of my late
mother intervened to save my life? I think not. And I'm not
grand or guarded enough to believe the close call had anything
to do with God. Yet, I know the small still voice within.

After Waiting for the Soldiers to Go Away

I walked past the corpses.
Scattered corpses littered
the street. Many times
before, I had come upon
such scenes. A small corpse
caught my eye. It was that
of a cat. Down on one knee,
I shut its yellow eyes.

Donna

Living on top of Wah's Chinese
laundry, they were Polish. Her
older brother looked Puerto Rican.
We called him "Spanish Eddie."
She was flat and skinny with lush,
straight, dark-blond hair flowing
well past her waist. Could've been
Rapunzel, but she talked like a guy.
We hung out in the same crowd
by the corner Carvel. She'd laugh
heartily at my wisecracks, and like
me, favored The Rolling Stones
and hated the world. I'd reassure
her: Nobody blamed her for Spanish
Eddie's suspected part in setting up
a neighborhood pot dealer for
a home-invasion-gunpoint-robbery.
Seventeen, she took no breaks
between lousy boyfriends. She
dumped the latest, a puppy-dog-eyed
snake (whose name I never cared
to remember) after he stole a roll
of quarters she'd stashed in the sock
drawer of the dresser by her bed.
Next day, it was just me and Donna,
smoking a joint, lounging in the back
seat of a friend's wreck. Her hair—
it struck me—was far better than any
tits, eyes, or ass. Hot and heavy—
when she abruptly pulls away. Says,
"We can't, we're friends." "Oh," I say,
"you mean like you just wanna be
friends?" "No," she says, "it's just
that we *are* friends."

For What It's Worth

As soon as the rock & roll
show at Young Israel
Synagogue ended, the 4
of us 13-year-old boys left.
Same stark synagogue where
me and one of the other boys,
Jules, were Bar Mitzvahed
the month before and said to
have become men. The rest
of the audience had gone
home, and we were now
hanging out right across
the street in the cold snowy
1967 Bronx winter's night.

Our heads buzzing in awe
after experiencing the Chambers
Brothers blast off and into
"The Time Has Come Today"
through stacked Marshall amps.
*And my soul has been
psychedelicized.*

The fresh-faced cowboys
with cute haircuts, who
closed the show, and surely
came from places where
there were wide open spaces,
now stood across the street
waiting on their ride. They
were supposed to be cool,
but they weren't loud enough,
didn't rock and the hippie
thing hadn't oozed in
from the suburbs yet.

One of our firmly packed
snowballs hit their blond
front man with the bushy

sideburns square on his natty
tan cowboy hat. If it had been
the nonpareil Neil Young
or Richie Furay who got hit
I'd be ashamed to tell it,
but I can't say I give a damn
about Stephen Stills and who-
ever it was who played drums
for Buffalo Springfield. Stills
& the drummer, both tearing
ass, chased us down the block.

When we got to the corner
the other 3 boys turned
right. They were lightning
and I wasn't, but I was cagey
so I veered left, and quickly
disappeared into a dark alley.

The next day, sharkskin suit
wearing stud, Jules, who'd
chanted his Bar Mitzvah
recital in tongues instead
of Hebrew, because he didn't
care about making his mother
happy, said the 2 Buffalos
who chased them were real
fast, tough to shake.

Tonight I'm at BB King's
waiting to hear Richie Furay
perform on his 70th birthday.
Minister Furay. Audience
friendly, Richie comes over
to our table, places his right
hand on my man Tony's
shoulder and asks if it's okay
to invoke a blessing. Rob
had told Richie that Tony

was facing heart surgery. I let
the wacky thought of asking
Richie about that long ago
cold snowy winter's night pass
as I watch hard-headed lapsed
Catholic Tony bow his head,
accept Richie's blessing
because he loves his music
much more than he rejects
Jesus. Elated from witnessing
the benediction, I am as close
to ready as I may ever get
to kick up my heels at tonight's
barn dance hoe down.

Ambrus Bohn

Hateful, small & manic, he was known as Bone, and fancied
himself a basketball player. Unable to drive to the hoop
effectively, or to pull up off his dribble for a jump shot,
he'd dribble-on aimlessly by the top of the key, and was a pesky
crafty butcher on D. More distinctively, in a cracked concrete
schoolyard of rusted rims, he had the foulest mouth.
His curious mantra: Eat me, eat me, eat me…

The Message

Had I known it would cost 5 times more
for me to get to the Long Island library
to do the poetry reading than what I'd make
from that night's sale of 3 copies of my book
I'd have done it anyway. Libraries are holy.
The neighborhood I grew up in didn't have
one. What kind of neighborhood doesn't have
a library? You tell me. What kind of a library
has a nearly non-existent poetry section? Most
all of them nowadays. The red light flashes
on my answering machine. I press play...

Muted message: male voice, my reading,
please call.... Alright! No one's calling
just to say hi you suck. Who knows?
A patron of the arts? A top publisher?
A fan offering pure cocaine? More likely,
the caller was a host of a reading who'd ask
me to feature. Maybe an editor requesting
poems for their journal. I'd return this gift
call after coffee, tomorrow morning.

Despite the message being muted, his phone
number was strangely clear. I dialed. He said
he'd seen in a local newspaper, that I was a poet
who'd read at a library, not too far from his
bookshop. "Who am I talking to?" I asked.
"Lou," he said, rolling into how he'd acquired
a fine poetry collection, but was having no luck
stirring up interest, so last night he called me
to ask if I wanted to buy it. Dejected, I said,
"No. Most public libraries have less than one
shelf of poetry. What *we* have has no value."

Teeth

In another time, in another place, he'd have been a kosher butcher
or a cobbler, but stubby-fingered Dr. Abelman was an oral surgeon.
Today, as I sit in his dental chair awaiting his appearance, my mind's
eye is forever locked on an image of him wielding a meat cleaver.
As soon as he walks in, he says, "This visit we complete your implants,
but before we do we always get paid in full." I'm a bit taken aback
because, although I expected a demand for the seven thousand dollars
I owe to be made today, I didn't expect it to fly out of Abelman's mouth.
I expected it would come from his attractive but steely receptionist,
or one of his in-house billers. He then adds, "After this, you won't have
to see me again." As if that in itself would be reason enough for me
to max out my Amex. Although, considering the needlessly torturous
ordeal he'd put me through, it probably was. Savoring the chance to
utter the four letter word, I say, "I've got *cash*." The promise of cash,
and the fact that I was already seated, moved him to complete the work.
Afterwards, I went to the reception area to pay. Somehow, he was already
there. Five or six feet behind the reception desk and facing a side wall
of file cabinets, the employer of two full-time clerks stood atop a stepstool
casually thumbing through an open drawer, the corner of his eye fixed
on me. I pulled out a wad of cash, snapping twenty tens, one at a time,
and handed the meager two hundred dollars to his receptionist, who now
cracked an I-don't-give-a-fuck-about-you-but-am-glad-you're-fucking-
with-him smile. Abelman turned toward me. He didn't wield a meat
cleaver, but looked so right in a butcher's apron. Blood smeared red.

2 Kennedys

As the station wagon began to pull away, ten year-old me chased
after it, extending my hand to the lean and polished, wavy-brown-
haired Bobby Kennedy who stood on its flat top and leaned
down to shake my hand, firmly. No one else was close by. He
had just finished stumping on the Bronx corner of Fordham &
Valentine. His kindness toward me made me feel that there were
great men in the world. Men who cared about others, men like
his brother, The President who was killed 2 short years ago. I held
fast to my encounter with him, keeping it secret to keep it holy.

Three years later, he too was killed. I was rattled, but imagined
that other great men would step in and somehow make it all right.
I ate the cream cheese and jelly sandwich my mom placed before
me, just as I did 5 years earlier after our third-grade teacher had
dismissed us, upon hearing the principal's muffled words echo
from the box speaker mounted high on the front wall of our class-
room. Regal and forever-dead, John F. Kennedy's visage adorned
more walls in Catholic-owned stores than that of Jesus Christ.

truths & other lies

say
your gym
teacher makes
you workout,

sweat a stink
dress again,

and next class
is the one time
per week you
sit beside

the girl who
rock 'n' rolls
your heartbeat,

you must lie.
forge a doctor's
note to stay
out of gym.

true love
trumps
squat thrusts.

=

say
you're a juror,
a kid drug
dealer's on
trial, you know
the worst of

the worst
thieves thrive
behind the great
wall of too
big to fail,

you get an okay
feeling about
the kid.

truth is
I deem him
too small to
fail, he ain't
taking your fall.

=

say
the man now
hiding behind
your couch
is on the run,

a rabid mob's
out to nab him,

you know
he didn't do
what he's said
to have done.

they're knock—
        knock—
        knocking—
on your door,

lusting to do
what rabid
mobs do.

you must lie.
say, he's not here.

=

greater truths
are often clear.

What Mattered Most

On and on my 5th grade
teacher Miss O'Gorman
gushed to mom saying
how fast I'd read *Jason
and the Golden Fleece.*

That most of my classmates
also could've done it
didn't matter
it was me she chose
a son of Jews 'just off the boat'
the handsomest boy in class
who quietly stood by his
modestly nodding
delighted mom.

My mom
who wished me 'pleasant dreams' nightly, mornings
served me tummy-warming crunchy French toast, who
wiped my 7-year-old ass when I got home from the hospital
after surgery to excise crippling rectal cysts, made sure I
never wore hand-me-downs, called me Tadeuszu,
protected me from hexes,

and who'd be dead
before I reached puberty.

My loving and gentle mom

who escaped the Nazis
only to marry a monster
who fathered me.

And I'd like to say her happiness
at that 5th grade parents/teachers meeting
even then
mattered more to me
than my puffed out chest—

But I'd be lying.

Biography of Blood Fouler

In the middle of eluding
genocide, he stopped
to set a farmhouse on fire—
after snapping the farmer's
neck, killing him. He'd worked
for the man, in the no-name
Latvian village where they lived.
Its straw-roof burst into flames
all at once. He'd say, the farmer
had bothered his sister.
No doubt he'd witnessed
someone snap another's neck.
At 14 though, he wasn't up
to snapping any robust peasant's
neck. Never cared for anyone
outside of himself. Whether
the farmer was burned
alive is anyone's guess.

In the new world,
his 13-year-old son taught
him the game of baseball.
He taught the boy how to tie
his own shoelaces and to smash
what you can't easily fix. His
9-year-old daughter talked him out
of his dumb plan for petty larceny.
He taught her rote multiplication
and abandoned her on the NYC
subway. The boy's bladder
was wrecked. The girl's hair fell
out. Both kids knew dad was blah
blue the old black birdy. He spoke
7 languages but had no friends.
When asked why he murdered
the mother of his children,
he'd say, "I did that?"

advice to my unborn son

if someone comes
to you with *the truth*
run

brush with baking soda
drink vodka straight
kick low
punch high
floss floss floss

find a job you don't hate

to deter a bully
saw stickball bat
in half
hide in bushes
flash attack
mercilessly

don't worry
pray
same shit

go to prom
escort homeliest
girl most likely to
recall it fondly

never watch sports
play
those guys
don't know
you're alive

any man named tim
        tom
        ted

who refers to himself as timmy
                        tommy
                        teddy
will steal the eyeballs
out your head and/or make
monkey love with your woman

eat no more than
2 meals a day

don't attempt to
handicap the ponies
analyze tote board
and follow
the smart money

tip starbuck's baristas
remember salvatore allende
stay away from girls named la la
never command anyone to
have a nice day

treat people the way
you'd like to be treated

if all else fails
become born again or hassid

make believe
you believe
better yet
if you do

The Love Fest Will Begin

Shrink touted Wall Street & Thorazine, but into poetry I fell.
Roll my words on concrete, our world spins in the sky.
A friend says the love fest will begin when I'm dead.

Snatched Shrink's pipe from his mouth, smashed it on my head.
Ink spilt on an empty page is a black cat streaking by.
Shrink touted Wall Street & Thorazine, but into poetry I fell.

An orange is to a guitar as a tangerine is to a mandolin.
In the beginning was the word, before the word became a lie.
A friend says the love fest will begin when I'm dead.

"I need a man to show me life," Maria said.
I had no reply.
Shrink touted Wall Street & Thorazine, but into poetry I fell.

Saul took a fall, got up, was Paul said, "For our sins Jesus bled."
Limp in the jaws of a low-flying bat a rabbit's devoured alive.
A friend says the love fest will begin when I'm dead.

Snatched shrink's pipe from his mouth, smashed it on his head.
Everything matters, but there is no reason why.
Shrink touted Wall Street & Thorazine, but into poetry I fell.
A friend says the love fest will begin when I'm dead.

White Knuckles

The past is the past, but it's always present
—Olga Maria Rodriguez Farinas

Twelve-year-old twin sisters Emily and Nan were away
at summer camp when their parents were slain in a suburban
home invasion robbery. The sisters were whisked from camp
by their kindly godparents, who raised them in the same
community, where they too, owned a home. Although each girl
had her own separate friends, they got along fine and shared
a powerful and consoling silent bond. At school, they continued
to excel. Occasionally, an adult or a kid would point and whisper,
cutting deep, all others seemed comfortable with the unspoken
taboo on the subject. The sisters went on to different colleges
out-of-state, where they married, lived, and had families
of their own. They did not, however, maintain any contact.

Dream Fisher

Dad tied a string to
a random stick, handed
it to me and said kid go
fish, before casting his
rod into the quiet,
steady country river.
OK by me. My Bronx
eyes, ears & heart
were flooded by the river.
I never cared to hook
a helpless flopping fish.

Back on the block
I could jerry-rig
a rod from discarded
wire hangers to fish
Spaldeens out of sewers
or work the wires
to lift a condemned
drenched & crying
cat from the sewer,
as the Clausen sisters
cheered blonde delight.

But neither Clausen
sister has ever appeared
in my dreams. Nor have
flopping fish, crying
cats or sewers, and every-
thing about my old man
was a nightmare.

Over & over, I dream
of walking a secret
path through the woods
to that river. Always,
blissfully alone.

Geometry

After handing out the test, our geometry teacher
the dreamy but serious Miss Martin gave out
chewing gum. That Juicy Fruit Friday afternoon
she stood up front and I found myself staring
at her. The crippling need to repeatedly order
random words and numbers 24/7 within my head,
eased. "Why're you staring, Ted?" she quietly
asked before the entire class. Clutching that rare
untormented moment, I didn't feel awkward
but stopped staring and shut my eyes. I got a zero—
I was too grateful released from being a hostage
to my own head to wrestle a hypotenuse. Since
the zero was an aberration, at the end of the term
she tossed it. But what I really wanted was to lay
my pained head on her shoulder and learn to cry.

The Mexican

Ahead of the crowd, I settle into a choice window seat.
This former school bus won't roll from Times Square
deep into New Jersey until every seat is paid for. I eye
all those boarding. They are, to quote Sly Stone,
everyday people. More than a few women board, lugging
shopping bags and little kids, and despite knowing
they will have to put their bags or kid on their laps,
they spread out as though ready to picnic. If I'm looking
for a seat, and need to ask one of these women to kindly
reign in her domain, I get pissed off. If I'm already seated,
I make damn sure my things are on the floor at my feet
or on my lap. Legs slightly apart, I will not budge
for any man. Always there are a number of larger than
normal (yes, normal)-sized boarders, and if you need
to sit beside one, or worse yet, beside a legs-way-spread
motherfucker, half of you painfully ends up in the aisle,
where you're sure to be mauled by fat asses, and battered
by bag after bag, at every one of the 10,000 New Jersey
stops. When a rare, slim, maybe sweet smelling woman
looks for a seat, I shrink, to make the spot beside me more
inviting. It never works. A regular-sized guy ends up
sitting beside me. The last person allowed to board
is a small, taut Mexican laborer. When he finds no place
to sit, he heads back to the driver to retrieve his fare
and leave. The driver, though, accounts for every seat,
and knows there's one remaining. He rises and waves
the Mexican on, escorting him to a woman seated beside
her small child, a woman who, moments ago, had seen
the Mexican looking for a seat, but hadn't made any
move to put her big-headed kid on her lap. Coldly,
the driver gestures for her to do so. As she lifts her kid,
the driver turns to the Mexican, but he's no longer there.
Silently, he's stepped to the rear of the bus, where he stands.
The driver gets back behind the wheel. The Mexican exudes
a kind of detached peacefulness, like a turtle sunning
on a rock. Everything I never learned about being a man,
I learn from that Mexican, this late afternoon, on that bus.

Unholy Melodies

New Poems

Last Train

I'd always thought that vivid memory
of me, mom and grandma waiting
for the yellow school bus that snowy
morning was my first day of grade school,
but it couldn't have been early September
because everywhere was milky white,
and I liked how the snowflakes licked
my face. I didn't mind mom pulling
my wool stocking cap over my ears,
but didn't like their non-stop doting,
as though I was leaving for who knows
how long, instead of some 6 or 7 hours.
Didn't know what to make of their wariness
of goyim, and disdain for dogs and cats.
Maybe this heavy snowfall meant frozen
hunger, most of World War 2 spent
in Russian work camps that followed
sporadic pogroms by neighboring Polish
villagers. Maybe before their transfer
to Siberia they witnessed Nazis packing
other Jews into cattle cars, families
savagely torn apart. Maybe that's why
my leaving filled their lungs with fear.
At school twin brothers took turns tagging
me and running away. I somehow knew
that these 2 weren't Jewish. I'm sure
that they had no clue about me. Maybe
a dumb game of tag was their idea of fun.
I was struck by their whiteness. So white,
they were cobalt. Their identical faces
bearing all the charms of a bare human skull.
I didn't like them. Then I didn't feel anything.
Then I knew I had to even the score. Then I
didn't know what to feel. Maybe the yellow
school bus was a last train to Auschwitz,
maybe I was supposed to feel scared.

First Time in My Life

I knew something was wrong when she showed up not wearing her nose ring. More than once, I had told Lucy Reyes how much I liked it. She had a broad nose. The gold hoop in her right nostril was alluring. Wavy black as blue hair, darkest eyes I'd ever seen, tiny waist, voice of a girl-child. So what if she was a thirty-six-year-old grandmother. I was thirty-five. More importantly, she had a tender heart, and we shared similarly rotten pasts. During our last date, a Cuban multi-artist concert movie called "Buena Vista Social Club" she welled up, leaned into my ear, and whispered how much venerable bolero singer, Ibraham Ferrer, looked like her late father. Afterwards, holding hands, we walked slowly. She says it's been 2 years since she's been with a man. At this point in her life, finds herself only interested in serious men. "That would be me," I say, honestly. We spend the night together. So I was shaken, when, the very next week, seemingly in a panic, she calls it quits. Incredulous, I say, "What's the problem?" "There is no problem," she says. "You're handsome and know how to treat a lady. But I've met someone else, a customer at the Vitamin Shoppe where I work. He's a veterinarian." Her way of saying he offers security. "Good luck," I say, meaning it. Misty-eyed, I'm actually pleased. For the first time in my life, hurt trumps relief at the end.

more advice to my unborn son

look both ways
before you cross
a one-way street

if a guy you're
about to fight
assumes
a karate stance
he can't fight

when you wanna
go fast
go slow

if you're lucky
enough to be a loving
girl's first boyfriend
do it right

you don't
need
a mirror
to floss
(first realized
the day
before yesterday)

if a neighbor comes
knocking on your door
to harass
you about noise you
don't consider noise
beat them down
with a baseball bat—
say they were trying
to push their way in

know the difference between:
maya angelou & meyer lansky

mai lai & michael jackson
your ass & elbow
charlotte rampling & rumpelstiltskin
agent orange & james bond
purple haze woody hayes
& the color purple
lay & lie
ugarte & victor laszlo

cherish the friend
who wishes you well
even when you're doing
better than them &

don't be dumb
enough to think
they number more
than one or two

don't believe
what patti smith says
on page 173 of "just kids"
she knew exactly
who sam shepard was
when she moved on him
at max's kansas city

if someone's good to you
be more than that to them

keep a plastic urinal
under your car seat

be very wary
of my trying to
do my life over
through you

RUBBER SOUL

That I was okay
at not quite 13
throwing
a make out party
in the living-room
of the small apartment

where me
my parents
& little sister lived
surprises me.

A badly-worn
green carpeted room
with cigarette burns
courtesy of my unhinged
asshole father.

That I sat there—
alone
a prepubescent boy
on the big-assed
plastic slipcovered
sofa bed

the portable
record player
that I'd carefully
placed on the TV

softly spinning
"Michelle,"
"Norwegian Wood"
& the naughty tit-tit-tit…
back-up vocals on "Girl"

while the other kids
sat on the floor
in a circle

playing
spin-the-bottle.

That I sat there—
tighter than my
double-knotted
sneakers

more nervous
when Debbie Z.,
a freckle-faced
redheaded cutie
with cat glasses

turned away
from the game
to smile &
stick her perfectly
wet pink tongue
out at me.

Yet today
I sit here—
alone

humming along to
"Michelle,"
"Norwegian Wood"
& the naughty tit-tit-tit...
back-up vocals on "Girl"

immersed
in memories
of arousal

whether I lived them
or not.

UPSTAIRS AT OMAR'S

Sitting in the barber chair,
in the closet-sized room
where Omar cuts hair, I'm
at ease. Soft-spoken, handsome
and artfully tatted, he rents
and lives in this house
with his wife and 3 little kids,
here in Jersey City. Now buzz-
cutting mine, I'm admiring
his new spiky pineapple colored
style, when he says, "Did you
have sex with lots of women
back in your day?" "Not enough,"
I say. "Women," he says,
"some who know I'm married,
come on to me. Do you feel it's
important I act on my chances?"
I'm surprised by the question.
He's a street-smart young man,
his friends likely macho, and me,
I'm a much older blanco Americano.
"It's up to you," I say. "As long
as you do what you wanna do.
Not what you feel you should do."
A knock on the door. His young son
enters, "How was camp today?"
"Good," says the kid. "We played
softball." "Sounds fun," says Omar.
"We'll talk more later. I love you."
"I love you too, dad." He exits,
shutting the door gently. "My father,"
I say, "was a violent psycho. You,
your son, and family are what's
important." But my father did say
he loved me. I was around the same
age as Omar's son. Maybe ten.
The Passover dinner at my maternal
grandparents' home, done. Everyone
remained seated around the table.

Sensing tension, I retreated
into the living-room. Sitting alone,
on a cushy blue chair, I was sad.
Slightly drunk and crying quietly,
my father approached. Saying, "I love
you. I love you. I love you . . ." he
slobbered kisses on my face. I sensed
otherwise. Something twisted and scary,
made me feel sick.

The Boy Who Never Came of Age

Summer in the upstate bungalow colony
is going great for this 13-year-old. His
brutal father remains back in the Bronx,
and peer pressure that hamstrung the boy
there eased here. Girls are crazy about him.
He's crazy about girls. Fooling around
in and out of the swimming pool, playing
pinball, Karen and Dory asking to see
his dick, apple picking, his almighty hard
on, being struck by a heady strange notion:
I can be me. But tomorrow is summer's end.
His mind echoing Dory telling him to meet
her at 7 by the jukebox in the lounge
of the Bollinger Hotel. Big brown glistening
eyes, she said she wanted them to *share
a night to remember.* Wanting his chance
to be alone with Dory more than anything,
he's game but jumpy. Same day his father
appears. After supper, Mom feels threatened,
asks her boy not to go. Unlike his father,
he's sickened by violence. But he's no
momma's boy, and swore to himself he'd
grab his Tony Oliva bat and bash the fucker's
head in should he ever hit his mother again.
No thinking. Swing hard, over and over.
Mom persisted, pleading with him not to go.
Eyeing his father, the boy, hot for Dory
and wanting to believe Mom would be safe
amid this cluster of adjoining bungalows,
is gone. A mile into the starlit night...

At the lounge, The Animals' "Sky Pilot" sets
him right. A sloppy kiss with lots of tongue
turns long and passionate. He forgets
he's nervous. She's lavender. Then there's
shouting, "Ted! Ted!" It's Nat, Karen's kid
brother, hopping around like a spastic
marionette. "Ted! Your mother!" Running
past Nat, into the blackness that minutes ago

shined all luminous and starry, he wants out
of his body, like during emergency hernia
surgery when he was a little etherized boy.
But he's in his body, a horse galloping
steadily, wanting not to get there…An adult,
he doesn't recall who, pulls him into a bare
room in a bungalow…left there alone…
thwack of a slamming door…. No one telling
him his mom is dead. And his father, the killer.

this has nothing to do with willpower

to kill germs
after handling any doorknob
you need to scrub soapy hands
under scalding water until
the world is a doorknob and

to kill germs
you need to scrub soapy hands
under scalding water after
touching anything touched
by unwashed hands

clothes hanging in your closet
need to be perfectly aligned

legs of the kitchen table
need to rest on pin-pointed spots

visitors are an invasion
you must keep watch
recall what they contact
as soon as they leave
those things need to be
methodically sanitized
and or put back in place

your heartbeat's not right

loud constant static
of exact random sentences
or number sequences pound
ceaselessly in your head same
sentence same number sequence
no letup no room for anything else

you are the symptom

day to day living
a depleting charade

respites very rare even
then you're nothing but scared
scared of your own mind
knowing torment's always near
running dodging ducking
what's not visible in the air

Rorschach Street

Slimy, gray & unflinching—
the rat I came across

was a cluster of leaves
wetted onto the sidewalk

Decoder Poem #2

When they say,
*Everything happens
for a reason.*
They really mean—
Better you than me.

When they say,
*Beauty's in the eye
of the beholder.*
They really mean—
They ain't beholding.

When they say,
*It's not about the
money owed,
it's the principle
of the matter.*
They really mean—
Money is principal
& they're looking
to charge interest.

When they say,
Practice makes perfect.
They really mean—
You've got zero
natural talent.

When they say,
Are you a smoker?
after you say
you have cancer.
They really mean—
Please say yes,
so that I can feel safe.
P.S. I couldn't care less.

When they say,
Call me when you get there.

They really mean—
Don't call me
if you have a problem
getting there.

When they say,
God never gives
you more than
you can handle.
They really mean—
You've suffered
irreparable damage.

When they say,
Based on a true story
They really mean—
Bullshit uber alles.

When they say,
You've got nothing to lose.
They really mean—
What you have to lose
means nothing to me.

When they say,
I don't mind dying
it's what comes before
that I'm afraid of.
They really mean—
All aspects of death
terrify them.

When they say,
Fuck you.
They really mean—
What they say.

SURVIVORS

*I believe victims of childhood trauma, even if they
have conscious memory of the details, have a need to
diminish the severity of their own experience in their
own minds in order to persevere.*

—Anonymous

He survived childhood trauma.
She survived childhood trauma.
What exactly?

Imagine the worst:
incest, rape, even murder

Similar only
in enormity of horror.

The kind where you,
the reader, after hearing,
tell yourself: I don't know
if I would have survived

Never did he have any peace of mind.
Never did she have any peace of mind.

They first met as adults.

She told him her story.

As bad as he felt for her,
he couldn't help but feel relieved—
He wasn't her.

He told her his story.

As bad as she felt for him,
she couldn't help but feel relieved—
She wasn't him.

MIRRORED

A boy child,
I stare
new-morning
wonder into
the tall mirror
on our foyer
closet door.

Mirror where
tight white t-shirt
topped, muscled
dad would
excitedly preen,

exuding a kind
of odd delight

befitting a being
seeing his image
for the first time.

Dad
who makes up
things to rage
about, busted
mom's eardrum,
and keeps getting
fired from
factory work.

Humming
Herman's Hermits
"Mrs. Brown You've
Got a Lovely Daughter,"
I march to
the bathroom door.

Locked—

I knock.

It swings open—

Void-eyed
dad
flaunts razor
above shoulder.

Says,
"I'll burn his house
down, the foreman
gets on me again."

And it swallowed me.
That moment

of knowing
in my head

what I knew
in my gut.

Knowing,
but needing
not to know,

the demigod
you're hardwired to,
upon whom
your life depends,

he's bad & crazy.

Nobody's Son

Down and out, I was done keeping up
with upkeep costs, so when my car got
stuck mid-street in a snowbank, it was
good riddance. Walk away, don't look
back. Deal with fallout if it falls out.

A car then pulled over, a man stepped
out. I'd seen him before, a middle-aged
black man wearing a red & black plaid
hunting jacket and cap. He scowled at me,
then went to his trunk. Took out a chain,
hooked our cars up. The kind of man who
took an angry pride in doing things right.

Looking into his eyes, I nodded thanks.
"Would you do the same for my son?"
he asked. But wanted no reply, and drove
off. Best lesson I ever learned on race.
But I wasn't the kind to help anyone. He
was somebody's father, I was nobody's son.

NOT VALENTINE'S DAY

To your head
from his hip,
Assistant Principal Carmody
would launch
a mid-knuckle-protruding fist.

Thirteen in junior high,
I looked 13.

Lots of boys
at that Bronx school
had already turned 16.

A hideous mosaic
from the bad to worst
of every race & ethnicity.

Closer to Nam or Riker's
than they'd ever be to high school,
these gap-toothed man-boys
bopped around palming
no more than a single
small notebook.

Laughing in the hallway,
Paul Noonan got clipped—
bolted into the bathroom
& kicked down a stall.

Slipping out a fire exit,
Marvin Barnes got clipped—
mumbled, white motherfucker,
under his breath.

I got clipped—
no reason.
Stayed mum,
felt like passing out.

Scuffling in the cafeteria,
Valentine Rivera got clipped—
& cat-leapt
onto Carmody's fat neck.

Trays, food & fists flew.

Some danced atop tables,
others got stomped.

Carmody over Valentine
by knockout.

FIVE CORNERS

Mr. Noveck must've been heavy
into the mob for cash, because
Noveck's Drugs at Five Corners
had no pharmacist. Running
the store, in '87, smirking, relaxed
wiseguys in the making, sold
pharmaceutical narcotics openly.
Over the counter. No script needed.
No street scenes. Self-medication
and highs, all in walking distance.

The low-lying often flooded
Bronx River area Mud West turned
into Five Corners, after the multi-
legged intersection at Unionport
Road and Victor Street was built.
A neighborhood where to this day,
you can still see many old houses
with retrofitted front entrances cut
into what were originally second
floors. Something I noticed
during frequent visits to my fresh,
easy-access connection at Noveck's.

Prior to that, I'd trek to Five Corners
maybe once a week, take in a movie
at an old half-priced theater, The Palace.
That year watching Mickey Rourke's
steamy tryst with pulse-raising nymphet
Lisa Bonet in "Angel Heart," Mamet's
sleight-of-hand plot turns and tricks
in "House of Games," and U.S. soldier
"Joker" firing a bullet into a fallen Viet-
namese girl sniper in "Full Metal Jacket."

Entering the warm confines of Noveck's
late morning one cold winter's day,
I realized I loved the place. Glorying
in its sheer audacity, very much aware

that like all laws, the ones regarding drugs
were arbitrary, made by men to rule men
other than themselves. After picking up,
I ensured a good quick buzz, swallowing
3 seconals on an empty stomach before
heading for the matinee at the Palace.

Astoundingly, a movie "Five Corners"
was playing. Released from jail in '64,
Heinz goes straight home. Walks streets
I know. And no surprise, targets the same
girl he was caged for attempting to rape.
Threatens her protector. Abducts 2
penguins from the Bronx Zoo, and clubs
one to death. Then visiting his harmless,
demented mom. Despite his teary pleas,
she can't accept and repeat what he plainly
says, he's been away in jail, and tonight,
will die. Finally, she does. He lovingly
lifts, cradles her in his arms like a newly-
wed bride, and hurls her, glass shattering,
through the window. A poor woman
plummeting to her death, and I laughed.
It wasn't funny. But I know, dealing
with a psycho anything can happen. Unlike
the storefront gate at Noveck's getting pulled
down for good, I never saw it coming.

AND SO I DID

New York City, circa early 90s

Sensing
3 teenaged black boys
closing ground behind me
I pause
to tie my shoelace,
let them pass:
3 scrubbed schoolboys
carrying bulky backpacks—
abruptly stop.
One steps up, says,
"You stopped
because we're black."
And so I did.
"You thought we
were gonna mug you."
The 2 others never budge.
They seem embarrassed.
I feel bad about it.
If I had more than a quick
glance at them
before
I'd have known
they posed no threat.
"Well," he goes on,
"we can make that happen."
I know this is a
hurt kid,
an empty threat,
but I also know
that it falls
falls on me
to take care of myself.

The Breakup

I followed her orders
and ditched her sick old cat,
turning myself into a reminder
that she had abandoned her pet.

Also, I wasn't handy enough
to fix her broken toilet.

A Young Man and His Girlfriend with Hot Dogs in the Park, N.Y.C. 1971

On the photograph by Diane Arbus

What's she up to, this strange lady
who I'm letting take a picture of me
and Gina? She can see I just bought
us a couple hot dogs, and Gina's
already started on hers. Well, what
the fuck, going along with posing
will show Gina I'm not always
a hard-ass. Anyhow, that Hawaiian
weed we smoked has me mellow.
She'll get that she's lucky, hanging
on my arm, because this picture's
gotta be happening on account of me.
Because of how rough and ready
I look in this M-65 army field jacket.
Vietnam, bona fide patches. And yeah,
I'm holding a hot dog, not an M-16,
and I've got long hair, but I ain't no
hippie. Don't fuck with me. Look
closely, you'll see I had to replace
the pull tab with a safety pin to work
the zipper. The jacket's forever.
A damn shame, my older brother,
Gus, whose it was, had to die.

My name's Ginamarie, but everyone
calls me Gina. He's the real serious
type, so I'm glad he's letting this lady
take our picture with her fancy camera.
He thinks he's smarter than me. He's
not. But I'm good going with the flow.
Besides, I don't mind playing dumb.
He's not bad looking, has a nice build,
treats me good, and always has the best
pot. Not for nothing, no other guy's
taking me out of the neighborhood.
And I like the scene here in Central Park.
Different kinds of people. I hope she

takes our picture quick because that
smoke's got me real hungry, and I
wanna eat my dog. Didn't even bother
putting kraut on it. I might bust out
of these bellbottoms, but I like to eat,
and he likes girls with some meat. I hope
he makes sure she gets us a copy.

THRIFT SHOPPER

Hunting,
I might find anything,
from a fitted shirt
to a wah-wah pedal.

But today I need to toss
a bone to my heart.

& am intent on talking to Rosa,
the buoyant cashier.

In a cold hand
I grip my cover
a dollar paperback

& detour past some joker holding
court sporting a thick, writhing
gold-specked snake coiling
his neck & approach her:

Alone,
she's humming
along to the radio—

Our dark eyes meet.

"Hi," I say.

"Hi," she says.

I say, "I might get a snake."

Her small sweet face scrunches sour—
"I don't like it!"

I say, "Howwa boudda Chihuahua?"

"I will allow one Chee-hua-huá!"

Dreaming our whole life together,
I smile and say, "Thanks, Rosa."

IN MY HANDS

"Okay girls," I say, as we
 cross the gridlocked street,
"let's hold hands."

7-year-old's hand in my left hand.
7-year-old's hand in my right hand.

The girls—
will be safe.

Gleefully,
looking up
into my stern face,
my niece says,
"You hold tight."

"I know," I reply.

Swirls
of rainbow sprinkled
custard cones
at Carvel—

One per girl.
The server asks,
"And for yourself, sir?"

"Nothing."

Going back:
I can't help but feel good,
whole, even happy,
as I again get to say,
"Okay girls, let's hold hands."

Why I Wish I Were More Like Tony G.

I know how much he loves live music,
but am awed that following a morning
of grueling dialysis, and an afternoon
at work, he comes into view, one foot
slowly after the other, drawing nearer,
meeting me tonight at B.B. King's.

Seated on opposite ends of a small table,
I'm glad to see that his face has regained
its color, and that he can enjoy a scoop
of vanilla ice cream. Having no interest
in the featured act, a rocking singer/guitarist
named Jackie Green, I'm here to spend
time with Tony, talk shit and share a laugh.
The man never complains.

Green, it turns out, is good. Sings well,
nimble fingers, and his band's tight.
It just doesn't add up to much. Afterwards,
Tony would assess the performance aptly,
saying, "The sum is less than the parts."

But now the band's rocking, Tony's eyes
are shut, head's bopping. On my feet happy,
I tap into his groove for half a minute before
my lack of feel-good staying power kicks in.

As the set winds down, the audience applauds,
and Green says, "Thanks." They exit the stage.
And it's all good—but for an encore. A cover
of the Grateful Dead's "Sugaree" that includes
a long jam. But it's late, and they're not the Dead.

Tony leans over, to whisper something
into my ear, I'm pleased to hear him say,
"This is fucking torture." Set always to escape,
and knowing that bad can only get worse, I say,
"Let's get the fuck out of here." "No," he says,
"they might play something I like next."

LAUGHING MAN

Sprawled, decrepit, on the pavement,
at the busy 59ᵗʰ Street subway entrance,
a beggar nods, wasted. Strewn coins
and a tipped red plastic cup at his side.

Striding by, a tall, stylish older woman,
barely pausing, scoops up some coins
and continues down the stairs. I can barely
believe my eyes. Trembling, the beggar rises:
"FuckinbitchFuckinbitchFuckinbitch …"

She needs shaming, I must give chase.
But I'm not about to break a sweat.
Instead, I laugh and laugh. This absurdly
base robber making my day. Tomorrow,
maybe, I'll feel enough to care.

The Lies of David Berkowitz

No way was I going to get sweaty in gym.
Not when next class, Spanish, meant sitting
beside the girl I desired most at Columbus
High School, Sarah Twist. Smart, pretty,
and Jewish. The kind Mom would like,
if she was still alive. On my perch in the rear
bleachers, planning to make her mine I watch
a Bronx mix of hippies, greasers, and misfits
lamely play volleyball. One player, I knew.
Big lug, rock star wannabe Bobby "Boosh."
Another kid though caught my eye, black
dress socks with sneakers. Before clapping,
he'd blankly look to others. Stopping only
when they did. Crinkly dark hair thinning,
he already looked like a middle-age schlub.
From him, I sensed trouble. And in 5 years
his image appeared on the front pages of every
newspaper and all TVs, David Berkowitz,
notorious .44 caliber serial killer AKA Son
of Sam, who terrorized New York City.

Thirty years later, an article in the Times,
the imprisoned serial killer expressing remorse
for having been a school bully. This jogged
my memory: After school, I called out to 2
boys walking ahead of me. They halted, near
a group of kids waiting at the parkway bus stop
for their ride home to Co-op City. "What's
happening, Charlie," I say. "Hey, Boosh."
They nod. Not much of a guitarist, he dressed
like a lean rocker: a 2-sizes-too-small tattered
dungaree jacket and powder blue clogs. His hair,
an intergalactic bushy shag. No longer having
Charlie to himself, Boosh gets antsy, twitching
and so forth. Next thing I know, he makes
a beeline to a lone kid on the outskirt of those
by the bus stop. The schlub from gym. He starts
jostling him. Berkowitz doesn't retaliate.
A disgrace, taking shit from a kid wearing clogs.
Shamed, a hunched Berkowitz boards the bus.

Why the lie? Same reason a guy I grew up with
says that back in his day he could slam
a Spaulding over a 6-story building in stickball,
when all I can remember are his pop ups
and grounders. Another denies eating chalk.
But I was there, third-grade class 3-6. Grinning,
he stood by the blackboard gnawing on the glory
of a chunk of crunchy white. Yet another says
he's a self-made man. His parents helped him
every which way. Serial killers, family men.
Makes them feel better. No harm. I don't doubt
they all buy into their own lies. They stare
at brown eyes in the mirror and see blue. More
power to them. So why must I be condemned
to my truth, never saying boo to Sarah Twist.
Prom night alone, shooting my nuts at Yonkers
Raceway. When I'd like to believe that I was amid
other graduates in Rye at the lavish Fountainhead.
My tux was gray. Sarah, radiant in a white gown
and high heels. The band playing slow and dreamy
solid gold, The Young Rascals "How Can I Be Sure."
Beating hearts, on the dance floor, hardly swaying.

To Baby Boomers Who on Mother's Day Post Youthful Photos of their Dead Old Moms

Everybody had a mom—
now's a short countdown
till *your* last breath's drawn.

QUOTES

Picking a penny up off the floor in the men's room at Yonkers Raceway, a demolished man says, "If you don't pick up a penny you ain't worth a penny."

"The trouble with you," says the barfly to the rotund bartender, "is you're overfed but under-fucked."

Telling her father that she's one of only 5 students at middle-school to pass the test to attend Stuyvesant High School, he says, "You've got a nice little body, you'll do fine."

Shuffling through a packed subway car, a foul-smelling derelict says, "Anybody got the time?" "Time," a woman shouts, "to wash your ass!"

Bitching to one more born loser at the track that had the photo finish gone my way I'd have won big, he says, "And if your grandmother had balls she'd a been your grandfather."

After he tells his mother that her recently paroled pedophile brother, who she allowed to move in with the 2 of them, was molesting him she says, "I thought he only does girls."

"It's a pretty good country," says a tattered old-timer, waving a measly $2 ticket at Aqueduct Racetrack, "if you know what you're doing."

"Someday," says the father to his little son, "you'll be eatin' out of a garbage can."

"I want to raise my child to be well adjusted," says the young mom, "but there's nothing to be well-adjusted to."

Overheard in my head: "I still consider myself violent and mentally ill, but as I'm all flight and no fight, there is no actionable offense."

FATE

Looking down at the gooey orange liquid
and jagged shards of glass on the sidewalk,
I damn well know that if that bottle of soda
tossed from high above had landed a foot
to the left it would've exploded on top
of my head. Sprawled in a puddle of blood,
I'd be too dead to be embarrassed about being
the sole winner of this lottery of the unlucky.
When a passerby phones the cops, I split,

and find shelter in the scrap paper chicken
scratch to-do list I pull from the back pocket
of my pants: withdraw sixty bucks Chase
Bank, haircut, half a pound smoked ham
and 2 Roach Motels at ShopRite.

Missions complete, I crumple the list and
crown it on a small mountain of garbage can
overflow, where the slightest breeze
will blow it into urban eternity.

Home, I place one trap below the kitchen
sink and the other on the bathroom floor,
behind the toilet. I'd rather swallow a roach
whole than have one crawl into my inviting
asshole while I'm on the crapper.

Lunching on the ham, I ask myself who'd
toss a bottle of orange soda onto a busy street.
Could be anyone, from an impulse-control-
challenged punk to the President of the United
States. Or maybe it dropped from the sun.

I then recall every step leading to my brush
with death. Anything seemingly random
happen to affect the timing of my movements?
Detours? Anybody bump into me? Spirit
of my late mother intervene to save my life?
My number simply not yet up? God's warning
to change my nasty ways?

I'm not grand or guarded enough to believe
the close call had anything to do with God,
so I asked Him. Here's what he said, "Son,
life's a mixed bag—a big con—the rest's
a craphoot. Don't take everything so
seriously and get your ass ready to die."

In Your Trust Dream

after Richard Hugo

You're trapped in a basement room
of a strangely familiar tenement. Belzer,
the only kid in your 5th grade class
who, when the teacher asked
what money was based on, knew
the answer was trust, is also there.
At his back, a slack-eyed teenage
gangster gripping a dagger 2-handed
overhead, set to plunge it into him,
sees you so instead barely slashes him
and runs away, leaving you 2
on a busy street by a traffic-heavy
intersection. You're trying to flag
bleeding Belzer a cab to the hospital,
but he disappears. Next you're on
the run, pegged by the gang for death,
desperate to escape this neighborhood.
Not knowing any vacant lot shortcuts
or alleyway hideouts, you're seized
by 3 gangsters, while trying to talk them
into you not being the outsider for whom
they're searching, Belzer reappears,
no worse for wear to betray you.

ALISON

As the tech applies cold gel
to my neck for the ultrasound test,
summer fun of 20 years ago runs
behind my eyes. The highlight,
a week-long getaway to Cape Cod.
Sex and more sex, the salty-scent
headrush and savage beauty
of the dark ocean, moonlight boat rides…
Whatever she wanted to do—sightsee,
poke around antique shops, attend
a timeshare sales presentation, I'd do.

Fifteen minutes of scanning my throat
with the stethoscope-like probe,
and knowing the exam would end in
a few minutes, I recall something
that I had never given a second thought:
Alison was an ultrasound tech.

Shortly past Labor Day, crying,
she broke up with me. I didn't ask
why. I didn't know if she was crying
because she'd miss me, or feeling bad
because she made me feel bad. No matter.
Her tears were arousing. I made my move.
She turned away. "That's not gonna make
things better," and walked me to the door.

Before exiting the room, the tech
tells me to wait right there. Dread
in heart rises into head and heavies
feet. No sign of disease. They say
you can leave. They'll call you
in a week. Waiting means a doctor
will make an appearance. The one
word you'll hear is *recurrence*.

If Alison were here,
would she have recognized me?
Would she have delivered the bad
news herself, stayed with me
as I waited for the doctor?
Would she have cried? I do know
that nothing would have made it any better.

the clown

jumbo red nose
neon blue wig
& enormous shoes

on a busy street
I amble

handing balloons
to passing
kids & moms

to celebrate
the grand opening

of a storefront
kiddie dental clinic

offering free checkups

which will be free
unlike

the sure to follow

costly
brain surgery

One on One with the Big Dipper

More awesome than the spectacular
pattern of 7 stars in the night sky,
it was, indeed, Wilt Chamberlain,
coming into sight, as I stood taking
a lunchbreak smoke by the bland
midtown office building I worked in.
Streamlined and broad-shouldered,
a shade over 7 feet tall, "The Big Dipper"
set insurmountable individual records,
and was easily the biggest, most
dominant athlete of my childhood.
Larger than life, in my world he ranked
number 2, second only to Spiderman.
Retired for more than twenty years,
now into his fifties, effortlessly toting
a large gym bag in hand, his gaze fixed
straight ahead, well above all others,
strides long and fluid, he exuded
the aplomb of a demigod. As many
called out to him in adulation, I stuffed
a sudden twisted urge to yell, Howzza
air up dere? The man was a natural wonder.
Seeing him now, I was able to forget
about the fat rent I owed the usurious
lord of the land, and that in ten minutes
I'd be back working a job I hated,
for a man I couldn't stomach. Fueled
by rare purpose on this otherwise dead day,
I needed to show Wilt proper respect,
so I pursued him. Standing by his side,
I said, "Wilt, you could still lead the league
in rebounding." He halted. Looked down
deep into my face, and said, "I believe
you're right." I was a little kid again.

Long Gone Lasting Summer

Unfazed by the mid-August sun,
12-year-olds me & Pete Boczek
played stickball & 5 Card Draw
poker in the deserted schoolyard
or would sit lazily on its hot concrete
backs leaned against the wall
sharing a smoke & my first hearing
Stevie Wonder's longing harp blow
ecstasy "I Was Made to Love Her"
blasting through his tinny pocket-sized
transistor radio. But on this day,
we rode our bikes into no man's land
1967 Bronx Botanical Garden
when I spotted a red-bandana clad
gang of black kids on bikes eyeing us.
Two aboard one bike (a dead giveaway),
all chasing after my 20-inch Huffy
& Pete's truck bike. Adrenaline
fueled, we pedaled wind. But one
of their solo riders caught up alongside
Pete who swiftly kicked the kid
off the bike. We didn't turn to enjoy
the sight of him crashing onto the ground,
but I hoped he was hurt bad. Two
white boys back in our neighborhood
wordlessly bonding.

Decades had passed, but that one-
of-a-kind crooked nose on a guy
ahead of me on line at the Edgewater
branch of Bank of New Jersey
was surely Pete. My lifeless mood
lifted & the bicycle run flashed
to mind. I approached him,
and was delighted that he right away
knew it was me. A firm handshake
led to a quick embrace. I endured
some of his almost instant pro-Trump
rant, before butting in to jog his memory.

Smiling, he looked me in the eye,
laughed & said, "Yeah, you & me,
Teddy boy, stickball & choking on
Marlboros, head-on poker, no-hands
& wheelies, getting jumped by niggers."
"Hey man," I say. "Don't use that word."
"I don't," he says. Then he launched
into spewing his hatred of The Media.
Boundless boyhood deep in my heart,
unlike the fall of our country.

On Dying

I hope
to die
painlessly
in an instant
peacefully
while asleep—
so I sleep a lot

A SERIOUS MAN

In spite of hour-long crawling
through the Lincoln Tunnel
into Manhattan, I can't say
I was in a bad mood, especially—
to make sure I'd get there on time
for a routine dental checkup,
I left an hour early. Besides,
the rain had all but passed.

Unrushed, walking uptown,
on Eighth Avenue, 6 blocks,
to the dentist on 48th Street,
amid the cool mist and early
lunch hustle, I felt good,
no longer required to take part
in this day after day tumult.

Throngs of salaried people
buttoning down. The rain
is done: A rumpled man
closing a beach umbrella.
A lovely woman clinging
to her purse, her 39th birthday.
A bank, a Starbuck's, a nail salon
doubling as a cupcake shop …

Angling through a crowded,
narrow, scaffold-covered
walkway, an open umbrella,
small and red, marching
blindly toward me. Half-stepping
aside, I swat it down—

"Are you serious?!" shouts
the woman, emerging
from underneath the umbrella—
viciously swinging it at me.
I block it with a bare forearm,
snatch and break it. She then

turns to walk away, and I say
something ugly—why repeat it.
I'm rattled. Not by her,
but my lack of self-control—not
for one moment had I considered
turning sideways to let her pass—
as I dabbed my slightly bleeding
knuckles with a handkerchief.

9 Things I Learned at the Reading Featuring Under-Represented Poets

You needn't be a person of color (any sexuality but hetero will do).

You can come from money and be under-represented.

Under-represented sub-categories are represented disproportionately.

Unlike cancer or death, there's nothing funny about being under-represented.

A white male poet of Hispanic descent can rail against the horrors committed by white men, including the *invention* of cannibalism?

The insane and crippled don't merit under-represented status.

A poet will write nigger, but not say it. Why not just read another fucking poem?

Over-represented tenured white male professors will be over-represented in the audience.

True under-representation requires an MFA degree.

despite sound sleep

I spot shadowy death
angling to unmake me
at the foot of my bed
but I mule kick & kick
& if that's not enough
I distract the intruder
jive talking non-stop

WHAT MATTERED MOST

Standing quietly alone
I watched
as my 5th-grade teacher
Miss Goldwasser
gushed on and on about me
to Mom

My modestly nodding
glowing young Mom

Who wished me
pleasant dreams nightly

Called me Tadeuszu

Mornings served
crunchy warm French toast

Who
after my hospitalization
for surgery to excise
crippling rectal cysts
wiped my 7-year-old butt

Made sure I never wore
hand-me-downs

Protected me from hexes

And who was dead
before I reached puberty

My loving and gentle Mom

Who survived Stalin's Siberia
only to marry The Curse
whose seed gave rise to me

And I'd like to say
her happiness
at that parent-teacher meeting
even then

mattered more to me
than my puffed-up chest

But I'd be lying

THE EMPEROR OF POETRY

Addressing our small
gathering, he says,
I wrote this poem
about Madagascar
while in Madagascar ...

Hearing him read
the polysyllabic pap
that is his poem
about Madagascar
while in Madagascar,

I realize my sole purpose,
introducing Mr. Spitball
to his well-traveled tonsils.

But instead, use the straw
in my Coke to poke, poke,
poke a floating ice cube.

Dear E of P:

Please remove your naked ass
from the stage and take your pages
of sure-to-close-any-open-mind
to poetry with you.

I hear the muses calling,
calling for you—

Please return to Madagascar.

old man blues

used to be
an over-the-door
mirror
was a comfort

nowadays
I no longer
own one

& when I pass
the small
mirror that hangs

in my foyer

take
no more
than a quick
sideways glance

never failing
to give myself
the finger

Swimming in the Mirror of a Dream

Submerged in still deep childhood waters
I watch a blue dolphin morph into a man
who thanks to wetsuit & gear swims
smoothly alongside a pod of dolphins—
I grab hold of his thigh—we're conjoined—
swimming among the chosen reaching dry
land dolphin after dolphin emerges upright
& erect like prideful soldiers or phalluses
onto schoolyard pavement then I step
from the deep alone laughing sadly
a glorious moment of hope that someone
anyone everyone witnesses my rebirth

Job Interview

Thirteen, I'm an insomniac.
A week after my next birthday
Mom's murdered.
Her killer,
he who spawned me.
I suffer severe OCD,
depression, anxiety, PTSD
& random paranoia.
Get zero help.
Self-medicate
ten plus years,
heavy phenobarbital.
Have nervous breakdown # 1.
Find a shrink.
Says, Get a job on Wall Street.
Prescribes Thorazine.
Have nervous breakdown #2.
Same shrink says,
Check yourself into the Psych Ward
at Bronx Lebanon Hospital.
Check your mother, I say,
into that hellhole.
Kick phenobarbital alone.
Work jobs I loathe.
Have nervous breakdown # 3.
Survive cancer.
Survive another bout of cancer.
And yet another.
Have been blessed & cursed
to make 64.
Am a published author.
And you, you motherfucker,
wanna see a résumé?

CONSOLATION

You can't remember
where you were,
what you were doing.

Surely,
you were alone.

At long last realizing:

Whatever happened
between your parents,

the parenting you got
or didn't get,

most everything
that happened to
& around you,

you didn't cause
& couldn't control.

The lady on the street,
pointing at you.
Saying, "That's him."
Plain dumb.

20,000 dead yesterdays.

And the wild dog
in your gut might
never be tamed,
but the knowing light—
in your head—

that it had
nothing to do with you

glows soft & warm,
& you choose to be grateful.

SEVEN MINUTES IN HEAVEN

I was at Food Bazaar, tossing items
into my shopping cart, when "Cowboys
to Girls" flowed soulful and sexy
from the store's radio. And I'm taken
back, some twenty years, to a make-out
party at Larry's, where I'm sitting on
the linoleum floor among a circle
of other 13-year-olds in the one-room
apartment that he shared with his father.
Pole lamp, trundle bed, portable radio
on a card table, and 2 folding chairs.
A gambler, his old man was at the track.

Spin the Bottle? Better. This Coke
bottle spin pointing to a one-on-one
make-out session called Seven Minutes
in Heaven. First time I heard "Cowboys
to Girls" was at that party. Moved, I
realized that a bona fide smash doesn't
need playing through anything more
than a portable radio. Thinking, how
cool, a spellbinding number by a black
group, The Intruders, about cowboys.
They had as much to do with cowboys
as this Bronx white-boy son of refugees.
As the circle shrank, I grew edgy.

Then Debra Condor grabbed the bottle.
Gave it one helluva spin. Rotating twice
before pointing straight at me. Debra.
Not Deb or Debbie. Condor. Not Katz,
Bonanno, or even O'Hara. Straight, dark
shoulder-length hair parted on the right
side. The way she talked, not at all
like she was from the Bronx. Debra Condor
was my all-American girl. I had no clue
what brought her to that party. I did know
she was from the neighborhood, because
I'd see her on the street and warmly

smile, softly say hi. Our brown eyes
shared more than a passing glance. Now
she was mine. Or more likely, I was hers.

The closets and bathroom, were already
occupied, so taking me by the hand, Debra
led me out the front door into the hallway.
I shut the door behind us. Holding my hands,
she leaned back against the wall, drew me
tight against her. I liked how she took charge.
Resting my palms on the wall by her sides,
she tasted like a cherry Lifesaver—
"What's going on here?" An aproned old
bat toting a bulging garbage bag destined
for the incinerator chute. I might've said,
sorry to startle you madam, but we're having
some whispery fun. Enjoy your evening too.

But no, "Shutdafuckup!" I say. "And mind
your own business." Appalled, Debra,
palms-to-my-chest, shoves me away from her,
and incredulously says, "Who are you?"
Same way my wife says those exact words
when I kick the door, days after I was served
the papers, "Who are you?" Sheepishly, giving
the same answer, "I don't know."

PANDEMIC

Her siblings had more room and money,
but she was the one to take in her wheelchair
bound widowed 85-year-old mom. Shortly
after, her own husband died of leukemia,
a loss she deeply grieved. To make ends meet
she had her hours at the supermarket increased
to fulltime. Then, a misstep at home, a broken
foot. She *was* over 60. Her foot healing
just in time to return to work at the onset
of the Covid-19 pandemic. Still grieving,
profoundly worried about infection,
and leaving her mother alone in the apartment
all day, she managed to retain good cheer.
That much was apparent from our phone calls.
When I'd ask how she was doing, she'd say,
"Hanging tough." Tonight, when she asks how
I'm doing, I'm honest. "Persevering, but I don't
know why." "That's a good reason," she says,
plainly. "I'm glad to wake up in the morning,"
she says, "and put one foot in front of the other."
"Because yours healed okay?" "Don't play
dumb." She takes a breath, and before hanging
up, says, "And don't do anything stupid."

last words of advice to my unborn son

if your mom says
your old man's
a soft douchebag
with no hustle
stay mum

learn something
about anything
fake the rest
everybody else does

rue the day hava good day
turned into hava great day

99% of everything
is a sales pitch
the remaining 1%
is non-existent

if you start a rock band
consider calling it:
the slip mahoney arkestra

create a film noir:
10,000 keys to nowhere

appreciate
language poetry that's
more compelling than
ornate wallpaper

know: the king of kings
who rode into jerusalem
on the back of a donkey
had a hooknose

make good memories
you're gonna need them
when you get old

if god does not grant you
the serenity to *accept* the things
you cannot change—I say
it's okay to *escape* the things
you cannot change

if *you* think
your old man's
a soft douchebag
with no hustle
think again
harder

keep your backbone
straight & take care
of yourself

Acknowledgments for *Spiked Libido*

These poems have appeared in *The New York Quarterly:*

Son of Sam
Tommy bolan
These Words Are of No Help to Holly

Acknowledgments for *Bones & Jokes*

Special thanks to the editors of journals where these poems and stories, some in earlier versions, first appeared: "These Words Are of No Help to Holly," "Son of Sam," "Regina Einhorn," "what goes down must come up," "Tommy Bolan," "Damon's Way," "Hurly-Burly Buroo," "The President's Daughter Caught a Big Fish in Kennebunkport," "Straight Lines," "A Better Man," "Third Floor," "Salamanders," "Redemption," *The New York Quarterly;* "Haircut," "Chinatown," "White Men in Sandals," "God's Honey," "The Essential Dentistry of Dr. Jack Kreeger," "Uptown Express," "Ballad of Caleb Belleu," "The Healing," *Skidrow Penthouse;* "A Lion is a Cow," "Simeon," "One Day in November," "On Maxie Off," "Kiss of Death," *Iconoclast;* "A Jewish Giant at Home with his Parents in the Bronx, N.Y. 1970," *Slant;* "Letter to Lori Waterhouse," *The Hiram Poetry Review;* "To the Light, Darkly," *Dirty Napkin;* "From the Diary of a Prize-fighter," *Web Del Sol Review;* "Grace," *Jewish Currents;* "the sweetest dream," "The Volunteer," *Main Street Rag;* "Jay Spenser," *Fight These Bastards.*

My gratitude to those who helped with these poems and stories: Robert E. Mills, Tony Gloeggler, and Sophia Howes. And to my friend and mentor, the late great William Packard.

Acknowledgments for *Run*

Thanks to the editors of the following journals and anthologies who published some of the poems in this collection:

Chiron Review, Dead Flowers, The Iconoclast, Lyre Lyre, Mas Tequila Review, Misfit Magazine, Nerve Cowboy, Paddlefish, Paterson Literary Review, Pedestal, Ray's Road Review, Skidrow Penthouse, Slant, Sugar Mule, Third Wednesday, Trajectory, Two Hawks Quarterly

It's Animal but Merciful: (great weather for MEDIA, anthology, 2012)

The Understanding between Foxes and Light: (great weather for MEDIA, anthology, 2013)

Thank you to Raymond Hammond for publishing this book. Thank you to Amy Foster for her cover design. Thank you to Tony Gloeggler, Michael A. Flanagan, and L. S. for their feedback on poems in progress. I've become pretty good at finding the right people.

And thank you to the late great William Packard for everything.

Acknowledgments for *Unholy Melodies*

A list of previous publications was not included in the manuscript that was sent by Ted prior to his death. We apologize profusely to any magazine that should be listed here, and thank you for understanding this rather unique situation.

Sincerely,
Raymond Hammond